TELEPHONE SURVEY METHODS

SECOND EDITION

**Applied Social Research Methods Series
Volume 7**

APPLIED SOCIAL RESEARCH
METHODS SERIES

Series Editors:
Leonard Brickman, Peabody College, Vanderbilt University, Nashville
Debra J. Rog, Vanderbilt University, Washington, DC

TELEPHONE SURVEY METHODS

Sampling, Selection, and Supervision

SECOND EDITION

Paul J. Lavrakas

Applied Social Research Methods Series
Volume 7

 SAGE Publications
International Educational and Professional Publisher
Newbury Park   London   New Delhi

For information address:

SAGE Publications, Inc.
2455 Teller Road
Newbury Park, California 91320

SAGE Publications Ltd.
6 Bonhill Street
London EC2A 4PU
United Kingdom

SAGE Publications India Pvt. Ltd.
M-32 Market
Greater Kailash I
New Delhi 110 048 India

Printed in the United States of America

Library of Congress Cataloging-in-Publication Data

Main entry under title:

Lavrakas, Paul J.
  Telephone survey methods : sampling, selection, and supervision /
Paul J. Lavrakas. —2nd ed.
        p.   cm. — (Applied social research methods series ; v. 7)
  Includes bibliographical references and index.
  ISBN 0-8039-5306-2.   — ISBN 0-8039-5307-0 (pbk.)
  1. Telephone surveys. 2. Social sciences—Research. I. Title.
II. Series.
H91.L38   1993
300'.723—dc20   93-17342
                                                         CIP
93 94 95 96   10 9 8 7 6 5 4 3 2 1

Sage Production Editor: Tara S. Mead

Contents

Preface to Second Edition

When I wrote the original edition of this book in the mid-1980s, survey research methodology was in its early stages as it applied to telephone surveys. Since that time, a considerable amount of new methodological research has been reported, with many important methodological studies conducted and reported each year. In particular, the work of Bob Groves and his colleagues (e.g., Biemer, Groves, Lyberg, Mathiowetz, & Sudman, 1991; Groves, 1989; Groves, Biemer, Lyberg, Massey, Nicholls, & Waksberg, 1988) has had a great impact on the way in which any careful and concerned survey researcher will/should think about the planning, implementation, and interpretation of surveys. Nowadays, the informed and prudent decision maker will consider a host of possible sources of imprecision in surveys—coverage error, nonresponse error, measurement error, and sampling error—whether contemplating the design of a prospective survey or interpreting a completed one.

The second edition of *Telephone Survey Methods: Sampling, Selection, and Supervision* reflects a good deal of change and (I hope) growth in my own thinking about the planning and implementation of telephone surveys. This has come as a result of eight additional years of experience with telephone surveying since I began the original edition and as a result of what has been learned and written since the mid-1980s about total survey error (cf. Fowler, 1993; Groves, 1989). Following from this perspective, this edition makes more explicit the guiding theme of the original edition: employing telephone survey methods that attempt to reduce likely sources of error (i.e., bias and variance) in order to achieve high-quality (i.e., accurate) results.

My purpose in revising the book is entirely consistent with the purpose of the original edition: to provide a detailed and *applied* approach for those who are, or may be considering, conducting a telephone survey. I continue to believe that in choosing the mode(s) by which survey data will be gathered, a researcher should, in most instances, begin by making an explicit decision about whether to use the telephone, or to reject it either as inappropriate for the purposes of the survey or as impractical given the resources that are available. As such, I believe that whenever appropriate and feasible, a telephone survey is the preferred mode of choice because of the superior opportunities it affords for instituting controls over the quality of the entire survey process, thereby improving the chances of reduced total survey error.

However, in stating this, I do not mean to suggest that the choice of survey mode(s) is always an either/or decision. As noted in this edition, *mixed mode* surveys, in which more than one mode of data collection is employed (e.g., telephone and mail), are being used with greater frequency than in the past. Instead of viewing the various modes of gathering survey data as competing with each other, the contemporary researcher should consider how the different modes might be used in combination with the purpose of capitalizing on the respective strengths of each mode and limiting the effects of their respective weaknesses.

Although several other fine texts address survey research in general, and a few address telephone surveying in particular, none takes as applied an approach as presented here. This text is filled with mundane, yet very important details about a highly routinized process for gathering data via telephone surveys, regardless of whether the surveying is done with paper-and-pencil or with computer-assisted interviewing. Focusing on the mundane and specific when planning and implementing a telephone survey is necessary if quality data are to result. Many persons who conduct telephone surveys do not appear to recognize the importance of instituting the level of control most likely to assure the valid sampling and standardized interviewing that should be the goal of all quality telephone surveys; or, if they do recognize its importance, many seem unwilling and/or unable to make the effort this requires.

Given the length of this text it was impossible to address all aspects of the telephone survey process. Instead I chose those parts—sampling, respondent selection, and supervision—that are not covered often in as much depth. In particular, developing quality questionnaires for use in telephone surveys is not addressed in this text. Rather, the text addresses how to institute quality control over interviewers' *use* of questionnaires. Developing a quality questionnaire will not assure a surveyor of quality data unless quality sampling and quality interviewing also occur.

As in the original edition, I continue to assume that most users of this text will want to plan and implement local area telephone surveys (e.g., a city, county, or state), not regional or national ones. I also assume that most users will not have the resources available at the large academic and private sector survey organizations. Thus, most of the techniques for generating and processing telephone survey sampling pools I discuss concentrate on the local level, although explicit attention is given in this edition to two-stage random digit dialing (RDD) sampling. No one should attempt a regional or national telephone survey until they have ample experience with local ones.

This text does not fully explain the use of computer-assisted telephone interviewing (CATI), although many references are made to its similarities to and differences with traditional paper-and-pencil interviewing (PAPI). CATI has seen a considerable growth in the past decade, and will continue to grow. However, it remains a relatively new and still developing technology that I believe should be used by researchers only after they have adequate experience conducting telephone surveys via the traditional PAPI techniques.

I would like to thank again Leonard Bickman and Debra Rog for the opportunity to write this text and the support they have provided. In addition, I appreciate the capabilities and research support of present and former staff members of the Northwestern University Survey Laboratory: Judith A. Schejbal, Sandra L. Bauman, Susan M. Hartnett, J. Sophie Buchanan, and Dan M. Merkle.

I also express my appreciation to Bob Groves who, although we have never met, has greatly influenced my thinking on quality survey methods, and to Seymour Sudman, who in addition to his myriad contributions to survey research methods continues to serve as an exceptional professional and personal role model to several generations of survey researchers. In addition, I remember and appreciate the intellectual stimulation and practical opportunities provided to me by Len Bickman, Bob Boruch, Marilyn Brewer, Margo Gordon, Peter Miller, Emil Posavac, Dennis Rosenbaum, Frank Slaymaker, Wes Skogan, and Mike Traugott.

Finally, I remain grateful to my wife, Barbara J. Lavrakas, and our son, Nikolas J. Lavrakas, for the understanding they have continued to show toward the time I devote to my professional interests.

PAUL J. LAVRAKAS

1

Introduction

Humans have a long history of being interested in quantification, the process of representing something in some measurable (numerical) form. Quantities hold intrinsic value beyond their mere symbolic representations of amount. Although in earlier periods of history there was less need for the average person to have a broad understanding of quantity, that need now pervades our lives. Even persons who consider themselves nonquantitative cannot deny the myriad decisions they make daily based on considerations of quantity.

Since historical times it has come to be recognized that an exact count or measure is not always needed for effective decision making. This recognition has served as a basis for the development of sampling theory. Sampling, or the process of taking into account only a subset of all possible elements of a larger set or population of persons, places, things, and so on, has long been implicit in human judgment. (This serves as the underpinnings of stereotyping, for example.) Much more recent, however, has been the development of formal methods to engage in systematic sampling, which brings us to those techniques thought of as survey methods.

Survey methods are a collection of techniques for which the most typical purpose is to provide precise estimates (i.e., measures that are stable with relatively low variance) of the prevalence (i.e., amount) of some variable of interest: For example, what percentage of registered voters are likely to vote for a certain candidate; what percentage of households own videocassette recorders; what percentage of automobiles leave the assembly line with structural defects? In these examples, one does not need an exhaustive measure of all possible voters, households, or automobiles to gain information on which to base an accurate judgment about who will win the election, the size of the market for videotapes, or the quality of workmanship at a particular assembly plant.

When survey methods are properly employed, the resulting estimates can be extremely precise representations of whatever is being measured. So precise are they that their margin of error is negligible, at least from the standpoint of effective decision making. Yet valid survey methods (i.e., likely to be accurate) constitute a relatively new and evolving body of knowledge, which may explain why they are so often misused and misinterpreted. Furthermore, sampling error is only one of many possible sources of survey error.

TOTAL SURVEY ERROR

In his distinguished treatise on the various potential sources of error in survey research, Groves (1989) makes it explicit that in addition to considerations of sampling error, a careful survey researcher must attend to methods that control and/or measure the potential effects of coverage error, nonresponse error, and measurement error. Thus, the emphasis that often has been placed on concerns about sampling error alone is "incomplete and unsatisfactory" (Groves, 1989, p. 13). Together, all potential sources of imprecision and bias constitute *total survey error* (cf. Fowler, 1993; Fowler & Mangione, 1990) and each should be considered separately when planning, implementing, and interpreting a survey.

Sampling Error

Too often, those who assess the validity and applicability of survey findings attend primarily (or even exclusively) to the size of the sampling error, which is a function of the heterogeneity of what is being measured, the size of the sample, and the size of the population. This source of imprecision in a survey is associated with the fact that only a sample of all elements in a population is studied rather than a census in which all elements would be studied. Thus, for example, a random survey with a sample size of 500 measuring a phenomenon that is distributed approximately 50/50 in a large population (say > 10,000) will have a sampling error of approximately plus or minus four percentage points at the 95% level of confidence. However, this does not ensure that the survey will have measured the phenomenon within four percentage points of accuracy, because there are many other potential sources of bias and imprecision beyond sampling error. Collectively, these other sources are often referred to as *nonsampling error*.

Coverage Error

Before one should reach a conclusion about how accurately a survey's findings generalize beyond the sample on which the data were gathered, one must consider whether all elements in the population had at least some chance (probability) of being sampled. For example, in all telephone surveys of the general public, those households without a telephone and the homeless have *zero* probability of being sampled. Thus, all telephone surveys are subject to the potential effects of coverage error if one attempted to generalize the findings to the entire public. To the extent that the phenomenon being studied is correlated with coverage/noncoverage, the accuracy of the survey's findings will be lowered. In the case of telephone surveys, because those citizens who cannot be reached via telephone have, as a group, lower incomes than the population with telephones, any telephone survey is likely to find somewhat higher levels of income and income-related behaviors among its respondents than exists in the overall population.

Nonresponse Error

Few surveys achieve a 100% response rate; that is, most surveys sample elements (e.g., people or households) from which no data are gathered. (This is due to a variety of reasons, such as refusals, vacations, and so on, that are discussed throughout this book.) A survey's findings will be subject to nonresponse error to the extent that the elements that are sampled but for which no data are gathered systematically differ from those sampled for which data are gathered. For example, if young adult males disproportionately refused to participate in a survey and/or were less likely to be interviewed because they were rarely at home when interviewers called, then any measure that correlated with age and gender (e.g., going to bars or playing contact sports) would be a less accurate (i.e., biased) measure of the total population due to nonresponse error. However, if the data gathered in a survey are not correlated with whether or not a given type of person responded, then error (bias) due to nonresponse would not exist.

Measurement Error

Not all data that are recorded on a survey questionnaire are accurate measures of the phenomenon of interest. These inaccuracies may be due to errors associated with the questionnaire, the interviewers, the respondents, and/or the mode via which the data are gathered (cf. Biemer, Groves, Lyberg, Mathiowetz, & Sudman, 1991). For example, a survey question may be worded poorly or the questions may be ordered in a way that distorts (biases) the answers that are given; interviewers may behave in ways that bias which answers respondents give; respondents may be unwilling or unable to accurately respond to a question; and/or, the mode used to gather data (e.g., in-person vs. telephone) may contribute to measurement error.

Survey Costs

As Groves (1989) explains, efforts to reduce and/or measure the potential effects of the various types of survey error have real cost implications. The reader should note the basic distinction between approaches intended to reduce potential errors versus approaches intended to measure their potential effects. It may be too expensive to implement procedures that may eliminate (or substantially reduce) a potential source of error, but it might be affordable to implement a procedure to measure its approximate size and, thus, take it into account when interpreting the survey's findings. (The more advanced reader and practitioner are encouraged to study and restudy Groves's [1989] challenging, but nonetheless excellent volume, *Survey Errors and Survey Costs*.)

For novice survey researchers these considerations can seem forbidding or even overwhelming. When faced with all the potential threats to a survey's validity some may throw up their hands and question the value of the entire survey enterprise. But to do so is to fail to remember the fact that highly accurate surveys are routinely conducted by experienced surveyors who exercise the necessary care.

The present text serves as an introduction to these considerations as they apply to telephone surveys. This discussion is not meant to lower the esteem that good surveys merit or to dissuade anyone from conducting a good survey. Rather, it is meant to alert the reader to the many challenges one faces in conducting a telephone survey that will be "accurate enough" for the purposes for which it is meant.

My message to the novice should be clear: Planning, implementing, and interpreting a survey that is likely to be accurate is a methodical and time-consuming process, but one well worth the effort.

TELEPHONE SURVEYING IN PERSPECTIVE

Surprising as it may appear to some, telephone survey methods have undergone serious development only in the last 25 years. Prior to that time the proportion of households in the United States with telephones was too low to justify the use of the telephone as a valid sampling medium. Once the proportion of U.S. households with telephones exceeded 90%, which occurred in the 1970s, it became theoretically possible to sample almost as comprehensively as with personal (face-to-face) interviewing. Telephone survey methods, however, are clearly based on the methodologies that developed in the last 70 years with face-to-face surveying.

By the mid-1980s telephone surveying had become commonplace, and in many instances is the preferred approach to surveying. It is a methodology that has achieved a respected status as a valid means of gathering information to aid effective decision making in both the public and private sectors. In fact, more money is spent on telephone surveys by market researchers than by public opinion pollsters and academic survey researchers combined.

Why has telephone surveying gained prominence as a means of providing accurate measures on some topic of interest? Simply stated, in most instances its advantages far outweigh its disadvantages. (As a supplement to the following discussion, the interested reader can refer to Frey's [1989, p. 76] delineation of the comparative strengths and weaknesses of different survey modes.)

Although many fail to recognize or acknowledge it, by far the most important advantage of telephone surveying is the opportunity it provides for quality control over the entire data collection process. This includes sampling, respondent selection, the asking of questionnaire items, and with computer-assisted telephone interviewing (CATI) it also includes data entry. It is this quality control advantage that recommends the telephone as the preferred mode for surveying providing there are no overriding reasons that rule against its use.

This text stresses the importance of controlling and monitoring the data collection process to ensure the gathering of high quality data that provide accurate estimates. No other survey mode provides this opportunity for control over quality. When properly organized, interviewing done by telephone most closely approaches the level of unbiased standardization that is the goal of all good surveys (cf. de Leeuw & van der Zouwen, 1988; Fowler & Mangione, 1990).

In the early stages of the shift from personal to telephone interviewing as the dominant mode for scientific surveying, many were concerned that the data gathered by telephone would be of lower quality (more bias and/or more variance) than data gathered via personal interviews. However, research in the past decade suggests that there are few consistent differences in data quality between the two modes and whatever differences may have existed appear to be getting smaller over time (de Leeuw & van der Zouwen, 1988; Groves, 1989). For example, Tucker (1983) found somewhat lower cross-interviewer variance in telephone surveys than in-person surveys. Groves (p. 510) cites findings to suggest that there may be less likelihood of social desirability effects (i.e., respondents giving answers that place them in a positive light) with "threatening" items when they are administered over the telephone versus in person. On the other hand, there is a trend for answers to open-end items to be shorter in telephone surveys (Groves, p. 512).

A second major advantage to telephone surveying is its cost efficiency. Telephone surveys can collect data far more efficiently than in-person interviewing. For example, in addition to no travel expenses associated with telephone surveying, Groves (1989, p. 512) estimates that individual questionnaire items administered via telephone take 10%-20% less time than the same items administered in person. Although telephone surveys are typically more expensive than mail surveys, their potential advantages for reducing total survey error often outweigh this disadvantage.

The third major advantage of telephone surveying is the speed at which data can be gathered, and thus processed. In a week or less, one can gather survey data via telephone that might take a month or more using in-person interviews. An even longer period could be anticipated using a mail survey with the necessity of follow-up mailings to increase typically low response rates. For example, with as few as 10 experienced telephone interviewers, working 4-hour shifts, upwards of 400 to 500 20-item questionnaires could be completed within 3 days (including allowance for at least some callbacks). If, for example, on Monday a mayor needed some information by the end of the week to aid in an important policy decision (e.g., how dissatisfied are citizens with police services and should she fire the police commissioner?), a good survey organization should be able to complete a quality telephone survey of adult residents and provide results to the mayor by the deadline. This could not be done via mail or in person.

A major disadvantage of telephone surveying, even when well-executed, is its limitations on the complexity and length of the interview. Unlike the dynamics of face-to-face interviewing, it is tiresome to keep the average person on the telephone for longer than 20-30 minutes, especially for many senior citizens. In contrast, personal interviewers do not seem to notice respondent fatigue, even with interviews that last 30-40 minutes or longer. Mail questionnaires also do not suffer from the disadvantage of respondent fatigue, as the questionnaire can be completed at the respondent's leisure over several sittings if necessary. Similarly, complicated questions, especially those that require the respondent to see or read something, heretofore have been impossible via the telephone; although with the advent of videophone technology (on sale to the public in 1992), these limitations may eventually start to diminish.

Other traditional concerns about telephone surveys apply to coverage error and nonresponse error. As noted earlier, not everyone lives in a household with a telephone, and among those who do, not every demographic group is equally willing/able to be accounted for and/or interviewed via telephone (e.g., the elderly). Thus, telephone surveys are at a disadvantage in reaching certain segments of the general population, but there *are* ways that information can be gathered via telephone about people who do not have a telephone (cf. Frey, 1989, p. 46), making it possible to reach them in *mixed mode* surveys (see below). In contrast, regarding coverage error of persons within telephone households, Maklan and Waksberg (1988) report that well-conducted random digit dialing (RDD) telephone surveys do at least as well as the government's large scale in-person surveys (e.g., the Census Bureau's annual Current Population Survey) in enumerating and interviewing all types of demographic groupings. Nonresponse error will remain a problem in telephone surveys for segments of the population with hearing problems (in particular, the elderly), although this source of nonresponse in telephone surveys may diminish as new technologies facilitate communication via telephone with the hearing-impaired.

Since the original edition of this book was written in the mid-1980s there has been significant growth in the use of and, thus, in knowledge about multiple-frame or mixed mode surveys (Dillman & Tarnai, 1988, 1991; Frey, 1989; Groves, 1989). These are surveys that employ more than one mode to sample respondents and/or gather data. For example, a school enrollment survey of more than 2,000 households conducted for a local suburb (Morton Grove, Illinois) achieved a 92% response rate by beginning with mail survey and following with telephone interviews and, when needed, with in-person interviews of those who did not respond via the other modes (Lavrakas, 1990).

Telephone surveys and other modes of surveying should not be viewed as if they were in competition with each other. For example, telephoning can be used to encourage compliance to mail surveys or to screen for rare groups in the general population (e.g., blind adults) who are then interviewed in-person (cf. Frey, 1989, pp. 24-25). Rather than viewing the choice of survey mode as an either/or decision, the modern survey researcher should look for ways to creatively combine modes. As Dillman and Tarnai (1988) observe:

Each of the basic survey [modes] has certain limitations that defy solution. . . . The joint use of more than one [mode] offers promise for mitigating, if not overcoming, certain limitations of individual [modes]. Mixed mode survey designs offer the potential of using each [mode] to its greatest advantage while avoiding its onerous weaknesses. (pp. 509-510)

Therefore, a challenge faced in planning a survey is to think how, if at all, the various types of likely survey errors might be reduced through use of different modes of sampling and data collection given the resources available to carry out the project.

THE TELEPHONE PHENOMENON IN THE UNITED STATES

There are two sets of factors concerning the phenomenon of the telephone that directly affect the successful (i.e., valid) conduct of telephone surveys. First, there are "hardware" factors that physically determine the ability to reach respondents via telephone. Second, there are social factors related to the verbal and nonverbal behavior of persons contacted via telephone. Furthermore, as telecommunications technology changes and as telemarketing and telephone surveying continue to reach out to the public, we are likely to see a continuing evolution of the social norms of telephone-related behavior as these new technologies interact with human dispositions and proclivities.

This section addresses only some of the physical and social factors. Readers interested in more information should turn to de Sola Pool's (1977) volume, *The Social Impact of the Telephone*, Brook's (1976) book, *Telephone: The First Hundred Years*, Frey's (1989) more detailed coverage of the telephone phenomenon as it specifically relates to telephone surveying, and the Groves et al. (1988) volume on advances in research on telephone surveying.

Physical Factors

Interconnection of Telephone Lines

By the mid-1940s virtually every residential and business telephone in the United States was interconnected, at least indirectly, through the Bell network (Pierce, 1977). Before then it would have been impossible for a centralized group of telephone interviewers to reach all households in the United States that had a telephone since independent telephone companies did not fully connect. Thus pockets of the nation would have remained unsampled (i.e., likely coverage error). With the removal of this barrier, it became theoretically possible for a telephone survey of the United States to reach any household with a telephone, regardless of where interviewers were calling from or where they were calling to.

Saturation of Telephone Lines in Households

Even with the removal of this barrier in the United States, the prevalence of American households with telephones as recent as the 1950s was too sparse to justify fully the use of the telephone for drawing a valid (representative) sample of the American population. Although this has changed within the last 35 years in the United States, this barrier still precludes the valid use of telephone surveys in most of the countries of the world (cf. Trewin & Lee, 1988).

By 1960 approximately 80% of all U.S. households had a telephone. By 1965 telephone saturation had increased to 85%, and by 1970 it was over 90% (U.S. Bureau of the Census, 1984). In the early 1980s, only Sweden had a greater person-to-telephone ratio than the U.S. (AT&T, 1982). AT&T statistics from the 1980s indicate that of all American telephones, nearly 75% are residential, although based on several RDD surveys conducted by the Northwestern University Survey Laboratory (NUSL) in the early 1990s, this residential/nonresidential mix appears to have moved closer to a 2:1 ratio.

The most recent estimates of the proportion of U.S. households with at least one telephone access line (i.e., a unique telephone number) suggest that the figure is about 95%; although, due to the problem of homelessness, the proportion of the entire U.S. population that can be reached via telephone is somewhat lower. AT&T put the proportion of households with telephones at 97% as of 1982; the U.S. Federal Communications Commission listed it at 96% in 1981 (U.S. Bureau of Census, 1984); and Frey (1989) has estimated it at 97%. Thornberry and Massey (1988) reported findings from a very large sample (40,000 households) of personal interviews conducted annually for the National Center for Health Statistics. That survey estimated that as of the mid-1980s, approximately 93% of the U.S. population lived in a household with a telephone.

As would be expected, those households without telephones do not mirror the demographic characteristics of the rest of the population. Not having a telephone is related to very low income, low education, rural residency, younger ages, and minority racial status. For example, a sixth of all blacks (16%) lived in a household without a telephone in the mid-1980s, yet 97% of all persons 55 years or older with family incomes of less than $15,000 (i.e., older poor) *had* a telephone (Thornberry & Massey,

1988, pp. 27-41). It is important to note that on many behavioral and attitudinal measures (apart from those related to income), households without telephones as a group do not differ to any great extent from the rest of the population (Groves & Kahn, 1979; Thornberry & Massey, 1988); however, these studies do not include data on the homeless population.

Anyone planning a telephone survey should consider these findings and make an explicit judgment about the potential error that this noncoverage may introduce into the survey's findings. For those conducting telephone surveys in local areas, it is important to recognize that the proportion of households with at least one telephone access line within a given area is not uniform throughout the United States. As of 1990, federal government statistics indicated that in 10 states, more than 85% but less than 90% of the households had telephones: Alabama, Alaska, Arkansas, Kentucky, Louisiana, Mississippi, New Mexico, Oklahoma, Texas, and West Virginia (Congressional Information Service, 1990). Furthermore, low-income inner-city neighborhoods typically have relatively lower rates of telephone ownership. Anyone planning a local or regional telephone survey of the general population should know in advance the prevalence of telephones within the sampling boundaries. Then, with paramount consideration given to the nature of the survey topic, an informed decision can be made regarding the validity of choosing, for example, a telephone survey over personal interviewing or determining the feasibility of a mixed mode survey (e.g., telephone and in-person).

The future saturation of U.S. households with telephone access lines is somewhat uncertain. Prior to the 1984 AT&T divestiture there were concerns that the cost of local telephone service would substantially increase and thereby lower the proportion of households with telephone service, but this has not happened as of the early 1990s. Nonetheless, telephone surveyors will need to monitor future developments in the residential telephone market. Furthermore, advanced researchers should consider the possibility of performing statistical adjustments (weighting) to offset the possible effects of noncoverage error (cf. Massey & Botman, 1988) on survey estimates.

Multiple-Line Households

Another issue regarding the physical factors that affect surveying via telephone is that of multiple-line households. This has an effect on telephone sampling somewhat opposite to that created by households without service. Whenever an RDD scheme is used for sampling, households with more than one telephone number will have a greater probability of being sampled than the more typical household with only one access line. (Note that this issue is not one of having multiple extension telephones on the same number. The problem involves households which have two or more different telephone numbers, such as home office lines, children's lines, etc.)

Groves and Kahn (1979) found that approximately 5% of their national samples of households with telephone service reported having more than one number; the vast majority of these multiple-line households reported having two different numbers. In a large 1992 national survey conducted by the NUSL, 14% of U.S. households reported having more than one access line. These figures also vary on a regional basis. For example, an annual survey that NUSL conducts of the Chicago metropolitan area finds nearly one in five households (18%) reporting more than one telephone number. Here, too, statistical adjustments can (and should) be used to counter the unequal probability of selection due to multiple access lines.

Other Local and Regional Variations

There remain other types of variations in telephone companies' services and policies throughout the nation that can affect the planning and conduct of telephone surveys. This is not surprising with more than 60 telephone companies offering local service as of the early 1980s (U.S. Bureau of Census, 1984). For example, telephone companies have different procedures for opening working banks of suffixes (i.e., the last four digits of the telephone number). Local companies also vary greatly in the cooperation they give to telephone survey researchers. Another type of problem is the manner in which different telephone companies handle nonworking numbers, which is a special problem for telephone surveys that employ random digit dialing. What all this means is that experience with a telephone survey in one geographic region may not necessarily apply when sampling another region.

New Telecommunications Technologies

As the telephone industry develops new hardware and software products and services (see Andrews, 1992), telephone surveyors must be alert to the need to change to methods that adapt to these technological advances, in particular to assure high-quality sampling and interviewing.

Telephone answering machines and related services require telephone surveys to make many more callbacks than was the case prior to the proliferation of this technology. For example, in the early 1980s it was common to complete about half of all interviews of the general public on the first dialing (Lavrakas, 1987); now, this proportion has dropped to about one third due in part to answering machines and busier life-styles (see Chapter 3). Yet despite the impression of some, the majority of persons with answering machines (at least as of the early 1990s) have them because they want to avoid missing calls, not because they want to screen and, thereby, avoid receiving unwanted calls.

Caller ID, whereby a person can see the telephone number from which the incoming call is being placed (cf. Frey, 1989, p. 247), is another technology that has been heavily marketed by some telephone companies in the early 1990s. If embraced by the public this technology could create an especially difficult barrier for telephone surveys to overcome if large numbers of potential respondents refused to answer calls from unknown incoming numbers (e.g., a telephone survey group). Yet there is considerable uncertainty about the legality of this technology—some regard it as a violation of the privacy rights of callers—thus its future remains uncertain.

Call forwarding, car phones, and other portable phones (e.g., a new "Dick Tracy" wrist-phone was in the early development stages at the time this edition was written), also create problems for drawing probability samples of the public. These are situations for which telephone surveyors must plan before fielding a survey. Looking ahead, one can envision a time when each person could have her/his own personal telephone number (such as AT&T's "700" personal telephone number), which surveyors of the future will use to sample individuals rather than households (cf. Ramirez, 1992).

Possibly the biggest technological challenge to telephone surveyors in the next decade will be the introduction of the videophone, which AT&T initially began selling in 1992 for a price of $1,500. By year's end an AT&T clone was being marketed for about half that amount. Depending upon the extent to which this technology is embraced by the public and the business sector, there likely will be a period of many years during which some portion of respondents will have this technology and others will not. What will telephone surveyors do when confronted by respondents who refuse to be interviewed via telephone unless they also can see the interviewer? What attire will be required of interviewers and what should be the visual setting around the interviewer? What effects will the videophone interviewing mode have on measurement error versus non-video telephone interviewing? What benefits will the videophone technology bring to telephone interviewing? These are among the many questions that telephone surveyors will need to research and carefully answer as (or if) this technology catches on.

Social Factors

With the theoretical possibility of being able to reach nearly all U.S. households via telephone, it is worth considering the psychosocial environment in which telephone surveys operate. As Frey (1989) notes, there are certain behavioral norms regarding the telephone that have traditionally worked to the advantage of telephone interviewers. Regardless of whether all persons living in the United States grew up in households with telephones, exposure to the telephone in the home has been so high since World War II that nearly the entire culture shares these norms.

A Ringing Telephone Will Be Answered

Although often taken for granted, the most important of these norms is that a ringing telephone will almost always be answered, provided someone is there. Granted, there is considerable variation from household to household and from person to person in how quickly a telephone is answered. However, experience shows that if a telephone is answered, the median number of rings it takes is three or four, and more than 90% of the time it will be answered within seven to eight rings. Thus, it has not been a problem in telephone surveys for potential respondents to allow ringing telephones to go unanswered.

However, with the advent of new technologies there is some indication that a still very small, yet probably growing, proportion of the public use their answering machines to screen calls they do not want to answer. Furthermore, as noted above, the Caller ID technology has been marketed specifically for this purpose. To the extent that any sizable proportion of the public come to routinely refuse to answer certain incoming calls, nonresponse and, thus, nonresponse error, in telephone surveys may become an increasingly serious concern. The interested reader is also referred to Groves's (1989) comprehensive chapter (pp. 185-238) on the causes of survey nonresponse.

Protocol for Terminating
a Telephone Conversation

A second, less obvious norm traditionally has worked to the advantage of telephone surveying. As Frey (1989) observes, it is implicit in a telephone conversation that it is the caller who determines the duration of the verbal interaction; that is, the caller had some purpose in placing the call and courtesy dictates that that purpose should be fulfilled before the call is terminated. Obviously, not all persons practice this courtesy when they answer their telephone; otherwise, telephone interviewers would not be refused, especially by those occasional "hang-ups-without-comment." Nevertheless, this latter problem is not a common occurrence.

However, experience with the small but steady increase in telephone survey nonresponse suggests that this general norm is weakening. For this it seems likely that we can "thank" the telemarketing industry for hounding the public to the point where they have begun to learn to "just say no." Unfortunately, many citizens do not differentiate between legitimate telephone surveys and telemarketing sales pitches, especially because some unscrupulous telemarketers employ a fake survey approach to try to hook the listener; this is sometimes referred to as "sugging"—that is, Selling Under the Guise of surveying.

Judging Veracity

Another assumption about the interviewer-respondent interaction that underlies the validity of telephone surveying is that of veracity. A naive criticism of telephone interviewing assumes that respondents often lie when they are interviewed via telephone, thereby invalidating the data. My own research (Lavrakas & Maier, 1979; Maier & Lavrakas, 1976) and that of others (e.g., Ekman & Friesen, 1974; Ekman & Friesen, 1976; Maier, 1966; Maier & Thurber, 1968) suggests the existence of a general ability of listeners (e.g., interviewers) to sense accurately the veracity of another person when listening to her or his voice and the content of the verbal exchange. In fact, this research also suggests that in-person interviewing may be more susceptible to deception, because visual cues are more likely to confuse an untrained judge of another's veracity.

Furthermore, logic dictates that there are few respondents who would waste their own time in order to purposely trick a telephone interviewer, although some misguided and unprofessional journalists have started to advocate that the public do just this to political polls. People so disposed are more likely to simply refuse the interview. All things considered, it is a safe assumption that most respondents, in most instances, are willing to provide reasonably accurate information when queried in telephone surveys.

Other Social Factors

As noted above, as demographic and behavioral changes occur in a society these changes may impact on the practice of telephone surveying. For example, as a larger proportion of the American population is composed of senior citizens, problems associated with aging (hearing loss, social disengagement, etc.) will increase for telephone surveys. If other social problems, such as fear of crime and concerns about the invasion of privacy, grow, then one can expect further trouble for telephone surveys. These are trends that future telephone survey researchers must consider and for which they must seek solutions.

Summary

Despite some increase in the problem of nonresponse, there are no insurmountable barriers in the United States as of the early 1990s, either of a physical or social nature, that automatically invalidate the use of telephone surveys for the purpose of gathering representative data from the general population or from special populations (e.g. business executives). This is not to say that telephone surveys are always the mode of choice, but telephone surveying no longer deserves a reputation as being inferior to in-person interviewing either from the standpoint of sampling or from the standpoint of asking questions.

BASIC STEPS IN THE TELEPHONE SURVEY PROCESS

It is highly recommended that anyone planning a telephone survey develop a detailed administrative plan that lays out all the tasks that must be accomplished and that identifies the personnel who will be involved in each task (cf. Frey, 1989; Lyberg, 1988). The following are the steps that are typically performed when conducting a quality paper-and-pencil (hereafter referred to as PAPI) telephone survey, that is, one not done via Computer-Assisted Telephone Interviewing (CATI):

1. deciding upon a sampling design, including identification of the sampling frame from which sampled units will be selected and the method of respondent selection within a sampling unit;
2. choosing a method to generate the group (pool) of telephone numbers from the sampling frame that will be used in sampling;
3. producing a call-sheet for each number that will be used in sampling;
4. developing and formatting a draft questionnaire;
5. developing a draft introduction/selection sheet and fallback statements for use by interviewers;
6. hiring interviewers and supervisors, and scheduling interviewing sessions;
7. pilot-testing and revising survey procedures and instruments;
8. printing final questionnaires and other forms;

9. training interviewers and supervisors;

10. conducting fully supervised interviews;

11. editing/coding completed questionnaires and converting data into a computer-readable format; and

12. analyzing data, preparing reports, and so forth.

Once the topic of the survey is determined, the next step in the telephone survey process is to choose a sampling design. This choice requires determining who will be sampled and how the sampling design will be implemented. This includes decisions about the population (area or group) that the survey is meant to represent, what sampling frame will be used to represent this population, and the specific method that will be used to produce a sampling pool (i.e., those telephone numbers that will be used to reach respondents). In PAPI telephone surveys, each of these telephone numbers eventually must be printed on a separate call-sheet that will allow supervisory personnel to control the sampling process.

A draft questionnaire must be written and then formatted (laid out) in as convenient-to-use a manner as possible so that interviewers' work will be facilitated. The sampling design will partly determine the nature and wording of questionnaire items. Along with a draft introductory "spiel" and any respondent selection sequence that must be used to sample respondents from within sampling units, the draft questionnaire should be pilot-tested to identify potential problems with any of the procedures and materials, and to estimate interviewer productivity (e.g., number of completions per hour) and the average time it takes to complete an interview. This is a very important part of any quality telephone survey, and yet the pilot can often be accomplished with as few as 20-30 practice interviews.

As part of the pilot-test stage, a debriefing session should be held to identify any changes that need to be made before finalizing the sampling scheme and the respondent selection procedures, and before printing final copies of the questionnaire and other survey forms. Supervisory personnel and interviewers must be hired and decisions must be made about the scheduling of interviewing sessions. Training sessions should be held for supervisors and interviewers.

Interviewing then begins under highly controlled conditions. For example, supervisors immediately validate completed interviews and listen to ongoing interviewing, thereby providing on-the-job feedback/training to interviewers as needed. Completed questionnaires are coded (e.g., open-end answers turned into quantitative categories), the data are entered into a computer-readable format, analyses are performed, and the findings are presented in whatever form that may be required. This entire process could take as short as several days or may play itself out over a year or longer.

COMPUTER-ASSISTED
TELEPHONE INTERVIEWING (CATI)

Similar to the original edition of this book, this revised edition is geared toward those who will implement telephone surveys using PAPI procedures. Although it may surprise some, most of the procedures I discuss for PAPI telephone surveys also apply to a CATI environment. (Note: CATI refers to telephone surveys in which a human interviewer sits at a computer workstation that controls the administration of the questionnnaire and also may control the sampling process.)

CATI can be used to control the distribution of the sampling pool, even to the point of dialing the appropriate telephone number for the ready interviewer. CATI has the potential to provide many types of statistics on interviewer productivity to aid supervisory staff in personnel decisions. CATI may be used only to administer the questionnaire, without also controlling the sampling pool. In presenting the questionnaire to the interviewer, CATI can make otherwise complicated skip patterns "child's play," can randomly order sequences of items, and can incorporate previous answers into the wording of subsequent items. CATI also provides for simultaneous entry of the data into a computer-readable format.

Some surveyors, including many in marketing research, seem to have rushed to embrace CATI because of its "high-tech" image without careful consideration of its advantages/benefits and disadvantages/costs (cf. Baker & Lefes, 1988; Catlin & Ingram, 1988; House & Nicholls, 1988; Nicholls, 1988; Weeks, 1988). CATI is not a panacea but rather a tool that when properly implemented on appropriate studies should improve the quality (validity) of resulting data. Proper implementation of CATI calls for much more than merely purchasing computers, other hardware, and software. It also requires a substantial rechanneling of the physical and social environment within a survey facility.

I hope that the move to CATI would be based on a survey organization's desire to reduce total survey error (Lavrakas, 1991). In particular, if properly implemented CATI should reduce (a) potential noncoverage error and nonresponse error associated with managing and processing a sampling pool; (b) potential measurement error associated with questionnaire item wording and ordering; (c) potential measurement error associated with interviewers' verbal behaviors; and (d) potential measurement error associated with data processing.

Throughout this edition, I will note where CATI procedures differ from PAPI procedures and, in particular, how CATI should be able to enhance the validity of a survey. CATI offers great promise for those concerned with minimizing total survey error, but it should never be viewed as a "technological fix" that eliminates the need for intensive human quality control procedures. Just the opposite is true: CATI allows for an *increase* in the quality control that humans can play in the telephone survey process.

CONTENTS AND ORGANIZATION OF THIS TEXT

The purpose of this text is to assist persons who do not consider themselves expert in planning and executing telephone surveys and to stimulate possible rethinking on the part of some who do. Specifically, this book addresses the following aspects of telephone surveys in detail:

1. generating and processing telephone survey sampling pools;
2. selecting respondents and securing cooperation; and
3. structuring the work of interviewers and supervisors.

This text is intended to fit into the series of Sage books on applied social research methods, which includes Fowler's (1993) book on general survey research, *Survey Research Methods*; Fowler and Mangione's (1990) volume on interviewing, *Standardized Survey Interviewing*; and Henry's (1990) text on sampling, *Practical Sampling*. It takes a "how-to" approach to sampling, respondent selection, and supervision in telephone surveys.

Issues Not Addressed in This Text

The text will not address in any detail:

1. how a survey fits into a larger research project;
2. the wording of questionnaire items;
3. statistical aspects of survey errors and their estimation;
4. a review of the ethics of survey research; or
5. the analysis of survey data.

The Larger Research Project

A person should be exposed to a general social science methods course or textbook (e.g., Babbie, 1989; Cook & Campbell, 1979; Hedrick, Bickman, & Rog, 1993) before undertaking a survey, be it with face-to-face interviews, mail questionnaires, or telephone interviews. Only with an adequate appreciation for social science can the strengths and limitations of surveys be understood. This text assumes that one has done this preliminary homework, has decided that a telephone survey is the preferred mode of data collection (or is trying to make this decision), and wants to learn more about conducting one.

Developing Questionnaire Items

The limited scope of this text makes it impossible to give any attention to the generation and refinement of the wording of questionnaire items. Comprehensive treatment of these issues is presented elsewhere (e.g., Belson, 1981; Robinson, Shaver, & Wrightsman, 1991; Schuman & Presser, 1981; Sudman & Bradburn, 1982). When using other textbooks for assistance in item construction, it is also recommended that consideration be given to developing multi-item scales and indices through the use of factor analysis and reliability checks on internal consistency (e.g., see Dawes, 1972).

Estimating Survey Errors

The calculation of estimates of precision, that is, a survey's *margin of error*, is not addressed in this book. This margin of error estimate concerns the magnitude of the imprecision that occurs when findings are based on a sample or subset of an entire population, even when sampling is truly random. As discussed by Fowler (1993), however, sampling error is only one source of total survey error, and the reader is encouraged to review that book in this context. For the advanced reader, the definitive, comprehensive, and challenging treatise on survey errors is the work of Groves (1989). The Biemer et al. (1991) volume on measurement error is highly recommended, also.

Survey Ethics

Both Fowler (1993) and Frey (1989) cover a variety of ethical issues in survey research, for example, standards on disclosure of survey results and on voluntary informed consent. In this text, discussion will be limited to ethical guidelines for interviewing, although in many instances such guidelines are based somewhat on a surveyor's own professional judgment. For example, what one person may view as "persistent persuasion" on the part of an interviewer, another may judge as somewhat rude or overly aggressive interviewing.

Data Analysis

Covering the analysis of survey data would require a textbook in itself. Survey data lend themselves to all types of statistical analyses including those appropriate for experimental designs which, themselves, can be incorporated into surveys. Contrary to what some persons believe, surveys do not gather a "special kind" of data, per se, that require special statistical procedures. Rather, surveys are *methodological* techniques that gather data that might be analyzed by a wide variety of appropriate statistical techniques.

However, a special statistical procedure that is sometimes used in the early stages of the analysis of survey data is *weighting*—that is, a post hoc adjustment of data to more precisely reflect the population from which the sample was drawn to try to compensate, for example, for unequal probablities of selection, noncoverage error, and nonresponse error (cf. Groves, 1989; Massey & Botman, 1988). The present text does not address this issue.

Using This Text to Help Plan a Telephone Survey

Of the various steps that make up the PAPI telephone survey process, this text provides detailed assistance in deciding upon the following:

1. What telephone numbers will form the sampling pool?
2. How will these numbers be processed and controlled?
3. How will eligible respondents be chosen and cooperation secured?
4. How will interviewers be chosen and trained?
5. What quality control methods will be employed to structure and monitor interviewing and other aspects of the survey process?

Generating Telephone Survey Sampling Pools

Chapter 2 explains how to produce a set of telephone numbers for use in sampling. The first decision one is faced with is whether to draw telephone numbers from a list (e.g., a telephone directory) or to use some technique for randomly generating telephone numbers. This decision should never be made for the mere sake of convenience and a major consideration in this decision should be how to best address the potential problem of noncoverage error.

There are instances where list sampling is quite appropriate, for example, whenever some "special" group of persons, such as clients of a social service agency or nurses or attorneys, make up the population of interest. It is unnecessary, wasteful, and typically inappropriate to employ randomly generated telephone numbers in such instances, unless the density of the group in the general population is high enough to maintain an acceptable level of interviewer productivity. These considerations are discussed in Chapter 2.

There are many instances when list sampling of the general population would also be acceptable for a researcher who has no interest in generalizing to the population at large but, rather, is looking for *within-person* interrelationships. For example, if a researcher wanted to determine the intercorrelation of gender and television show preferences, sampling from a telephone directory may yield unbiased findings.

Conversely, list sampling is rarely appropriate if one's intention is to generalize sample results to the general public, because few, if any, lists of telephone numbers provide a representative sampling frame of the public. The only exception may be in some rural areas, where nearly all residents list their telephone numbers in the local directory and population ingress is so low as to alleviate worry about new listings that are missing from the most recent telephone book. In most general population telephone surveys, however, some form of RDD should be employed. There are a number of different RDD choices, as described in Chapter 2.

Controlling Sampling Pools

Once a researcher has determined the method by which the sampling pool of telephone numbers (the group of telephone numbers interviewers actually will dial) will be generated, attention next focuses on the process by which the dialing of these numbers will be organized and controlled. People naive to this aspect of quality telephone surveying may assume that interviewers simply dial one number after another until the desired number of completed interviews is attained. As discussed in Chapter 3, tight control over the *processing* of the sampling pool is necessary for quality (i.e., representative) results. Chapter 3 presents a highly structured, hand-sorted approach to controlling a PAPI telephone survey sampling pool, in particular so as to lessen the likelihood of nonresponse errors.

Choosing Eligible Respondents and Securing Cooperation

Chapter 4 addresses the second stage of the interviewing process: identifying and then gaining the compliance of the proper respondent. Here again, people naive to quality telephone survey methods often assume that interviewers simply administer the questionnaire to the first person who answers the telephone, not recognizing that gender, age, and other biases often result when such an approach is used.

In some instances, respondent selection is a fait accompli, as when one is directly sampling respondents by name from a list. But in other instances telephone numbers provide the entrée and names of respondents are not known in advance of the call. When this happens it is most likely that a surveyor will want to employ a systematic selection procedure in order to avoid the bias that could occur from respondent selection solely left to the discretion of interviewers. Systematic respondent selection procedures increase the representativeness (external validity) of the final sample by reducing possible within-unit noncoverage errors.

Interviewers and Supervision

Chapters 5 and 6 discuss the training and supervision of interviewers. Good telephone interviewers appear to have a natural aptitude for the work; thus, the recruitment, training, and supervisory procedures that one utilizes should ideally screen for and reinforce this aptitude. Although training prior to the start of actual surveying is desirable, necessary, and important, as explained in Chapter 5, routine on-the-job training is even more critical in order to reduce the possible effects of measurement error attributable to interviewers' behaviors.

There should be no doubt that the control afforded by centralized telephone interviewing over the interviewing process is one of the most compelling reasons for choosing telephone surveying whenever it is appropriate for one's survey purpose. The supervisory routine that is instituted over the interviewing process may be the most critical aspect for producing quality telephone surveys. Chapter 6 discusses the supervisory duties that occur at various stages of the survey process.

Summary

Whereas market researchers, academics, the media, and government agencies traditionally have been associated with the conduct of surveys, we have entered an era in which survey data is being collected to aid in all sorts of decisions made by policymakers in both the public and private sectors. This text is explicitly written with such an "applied" audience in mind. It is meant to help nonexperts learn to conduct, interpret, and evaluate quality telephone surveys.

ADDITIONAL SOURCES OF INSTRUCTION ON SURVEY METHODOLOGIES

Other textbooks cover the topics of sampling, respondent selection, and supervision in telephone surveys, but none covers them with as detailed a how-to perspective as the present text. For the most part this approach to telephone surveying is basically similar to that of others (e.g., Dillman, 1978; Frey, 1989). But no other author appears to place as much explicit emphasis on the importance of *constant and intense supervision* over the entire telephone surveying process.

Furthermore, a number of authors of survey methods textbooks developed their own expertise from experience with household probability sampling for use with face-to-face interviewing. I believe that this legacy of experience with personal interviewing has occasionally yielded a somewhat negative disposition toward telephone surveying, which is carried forward in the tone of some other textbooks.

As noted earlier, this text cannot cover all aspects of the telephone survey process due to its length. This is especially true for questionnaire development. Thus this chapter finishes with a brief review of additional sources for those interested in expanding their knowledge base.

General Survey Methods

Ideally, one should have a broad understanding of survey methods, not merely those related to a specific mode of data collection (e.g., via telephone). Babbie's (1989) text, *The Practice of Social Research*, does a good job of putting traditional survey methodology in perspective with other data collection approaches (e.g., content analysis, observational methods, etc.), as does Hedrick et al.'s (1993) *Applied Research Design*. *Survey Research Methods* by Fowler (1993) provides a comprehensive overview of almost all issues that confront survey researchers, as well as dealing with important topics that have received relatively little coverage elsewhere. Dillman's (1978) book, *Mail and Telephone Surveys: The Total Design Method*, is a very detailed presentation of the author's own tailored approach to survey research, including mixed mode techniques. In addition, Frey's (1989) text, *Survey Research by Telephone*, is recommended because of its broadly focused perspective on telephone surveying.

Every advanced student and practitioner should be familiar also with a recent series of volumes containing a wealth of chapters on various aspects of total survey error: *Telephone Survey Methodology* (Groves et al., 1988), *Survey Errors and Survey Costs* (Groves, 1989), and *Measurement Errors in Surveys* (Biemer et al., 1991).

Sampling

From a statistical standpoint, Cochran's (1977) *Sampling Techniques* presents an exhaustive treatment of sampling theory for survey research. From a more applied but nevertheless comprehensive perspective, Sudman's (1976) text, *Applied Sampling*, should be consulted, as should Henry's (1990) *Practical Sampling*, which presents an applied guide for the novice surveyor. Finally, a somewhat dated, but extremely comprehensive and still useful classic is *Survey Sampling* by Kish (1965). This latter book is "dated" in the sense that it was written before RDD was an accepted sampling technique.

Question Formulation

Although the construction of valid questionnaire items includes the use of scientific methods, the process is still somewhat of a craft and an art. As noted below, some texts teach the systematic steps that should be followed in developing new items for surveys. Yet the exact wording that is decided upon will often rest on the professional judgment of the individual surveyor. Of course, over the years, many standardized questions and scales have been devised and should be used whenever appropriate (i.e., a literature search will often avoid "reinventing the wheel"). Conversely, I am not suggesting that there is no room for improving on traditional measures. In fact, a surveyor often faces the difficult choice of wanting to use an item that has been used in a previous survey, thus providing comparative data, but regarding the original item's wording flawed. Unfortunately, if one "improves" upon (i.e., changes) the item's wording, comparability to previous data is often lost.

Sudman and Bradburn have collaborated on three books which focus on various aspects of questionnaire design: *Response Effects in Surveys* (1974), *Improving Interview Method and Questionnaire Design* (1979), and

Asking Questions (1982). Schuman and Presser's (1981) text, *Questions and Answers in Attitude Surveys*, can also be recommended for its very thorough treatment of survey item formulation. Finally, when searching for a collection of items that have been at least partially validated, compendia such as Robinson, Shaver, and Wrightsman's (1991) *Measures of Personality and Social Psychological Attitudes*, can be consulted.

For the advanced student and practitioner I also recommend familiarity with the review article by Bradburn and Sudman (1991) along with other chapters in that edited volume (Biemer et al., 1991) on the role of the questionnaire in measurement error.

Methodological Periodicals

A final source that should be regularly checked by those interested in telephone survey methods is the literature that is published in scholarly journals. *Public Opinion Quarterly, Survey Methodology*, the *Journal of Official Statistics*, and the *Journal of Marketing Research* are sources that often contain the better methodological articles on telephone surveying and survey methods in general. Each is likely to be available at any university library.

EXERCISES

Exercise 1.1: Review at least one other textbook that discusses the advantages and disadvantages of telephone surveys compared with other forms of surveying. Write a two-page paper comparing the position taken in the present text with that of the other author(s).

Exercise 1.2: Call your local telephone company and try to get information about the number of residential access lines in some local municipality and the proportion of unlisted telephone numbers in that municipality. In dealing with the company representatives be polite, yet persistent (if necessary). Regardless of whether you get the information, write a short paper describing the nature of the assistance you received (or did not receive) from the telephone company representatives. (If you are given the information you request please send a thank-you letter to the person who helped you.)

Exercise 1.3: Develop a comprehensive administrative outline, including a time-line, for conducting a telephone survey, starting with the choice of a sampling design. Assume that interviewing will last 3 weeks and that 1,000 interviews will be completed.

Exercise 1.4: Find and review a recent article on telephone survey methods from a journal (i.e., not merely an article about a survey that was conducted via telephone). Write a two-page summary of the article.

Exercise 1.5: Write a two-page paper on the concept of total survey error as applied to telephone surveys of the general public.

2

Generating Telephone Survey Sampling Pools

The concept of a sampling pool is not often addressed in the survey methods literature. A naive observer might assume, for example, that a survey in which 1,000 persons were interviewed contacted only these persons and no others to interview. This is almost never the case due to many reasons, including the problem of nonresponse. Thus, a surveyor is faced with the reality of often needing many more telephone numbers for interviewers to dial than the total number of completed interviews that the survey requires.

The purpose of this chapter is to familiarize the reader with various techniques for generating a telephone survey sampling pool. A sampling pool is the entire set of telephone numbers that will be used by interviewers to attain the desired number of completions (the final sample). Many important decisions should be made about the sampling design before a sampling pool is created. When a surveyor does not have a full-scale CATI system to generate and control the set of telephone numbers used in the survey, the entire sampling pool should be generated before interviewing begins.

The chapter begins with a discussion of the considerations that go into choosing a valid sampling design in telephone surveys. This decision must be made before deciding how to generate the sampling pool, because the sampling design guides the surveyor in generating the sampling pool. Once a sampling design is chosen the decision can be made whether to generate the sampling pool via list sampling, through random digit dialing, or by using a combined or mixed mode method, and whether to do this manually or with a computer. Several approaches to these various techniques are discussed. The chapter concludes by answering the question of how large a sampling pool to generate. (Chapter 2 focuses on creating sampling pools; Chapter 3 deals with the processing of the telephone numbers that have been created.)

CHOOSING A VALID SAMPLING DESIGN

Henry (1990) provides comprehensive, concise, and practical guidance for making sampling design decisions. Before fielding a survey, a researcher should make careful and explicit presampling, sampling, and postsampling decisions (see Henry, pp. 47-58). These decisions should include an explicit identification of (a) the *population of inference* (i.e., the group, setting, and time for which the findings are intended to generalize); (b) the *target population* (i.e., the finite population that is surveyed); (c) the *frame population* or *sampling frame* (i.e., the operationalization, oftentimes in list form, of the target population); (d) the method by which a sampling pool will be created; and (e) the size of the final sample (see Groves, 1989, pp. 81-132; Henry, 1990; Kish, 1965).

As part of this decision-making process, a surveyor must choose between the use of a probability or nonprobability sample. As Henry (1990) notes, the great advantage of probability samples is that "the bias and likely error stemming from [their use] can be rigorously examined and estimated; [not so] for nonprobability samples" (p. 32). That is, it is only for probability samples that the portion of total survey error that is due to sampling error can be quantified. Unlike nonprobability sampling, a probability sample provides every element in the sampling frame a chance of selection (i.e., a known nonzero probability). When this preselection probability is unequal the surveyor can make precise postsurvey adjustments (weighting) to compensate.

There are several types of probability samples: simple random, systematic, stratified, cluster, and multistage (see Henry, 1990, pp. 95-116). Although an explicit and detailed explanation of their differences is not presented here, this chapter and Chapter 3 discuss various applied aspects of different types of probability samples through the examples presented. A surveyor will not always need a probability sample, although it is very important to recognize the limitations of nonprobability sampling. The reader is referred to Henry (1990, pp. 17-25) for an explanation and discussion of the limitations of the different types of nonprobability samples (convenience, most similar/most dissimilar, typical case, critical case, snowball, and quota samples). Commonplace and typically appropriate use of nonprobability sampling is in the early stages of a long-term research project and during pilot testing.

In deciding upon a valid sampling design and the method one will employ to operationalize that design for telephone surveys, a surveyor must consider the following:

1. What is the purpose of the survey?
2. Who will be sampled?
3. How prevalent are "missing" telephone numbers?
4. What resources are available to support the survey?

Purpose of the Survey

The purpose of a survey is the paramount factor in determining the adequacy of a sampling design. Too often inadequately funded surveys are conducted that do not meet the purposes for which they are intended. This happens when researchers and survey sponsors do not (e.g., due to carelessness or time constraints) or cannot (e.g., due to lack of knowledge and training) think critically about the "bang" they will get "for their buck." The bottom line for any survey decision maker should be this: *If a survey is unlikely to provide valid information it should not be conducted.*

Most persons considering the use of a telephone survey (or any survey) will have one of three purposes in mind:

Measuring Population Parameters

A surveyor may want to determine the level at which some variable exists within a population. For example, what proportion of females and males have been sexually harassed at work? Or, what is the percentage of households with cable television? Or, do the majority of taxpayers favor or oppose an increase in school-support taxes? In these cases it is of utmost importance that a probability sampling design be chosen so as to contribute to the representativeness, and thus validity, of the gathered data and to allow for the computation of sampling error. The reader is reminded that selection of probability sampling alone will not guarantee an accurate survey: The surveyor must also be concerned about noncoverage (e.g., using a sampling frame that omits a portion of the target population) and nonresponse (e.g., experiencing too high a refusal rate), as well as other potential sources of total survey error.

When this is the purpose of a survey, the primary consideration is the *generalizability* of the sample, or what social science methodologists call the survey's *external validity* (cf. Campbell & Stanley, 1966; Cook & Campbell, 1979). In most instances if a sample is meant to estimate the level at which some variable exists within a population and the sampling design does not have high external validity, there can be little justification for its use. When respondents are sampled in an uncontrolled, unsystematic manner, as is the case in many nonprobability sampling schemes, there is no way of estimating the survey's sampling error. Without this estimate of statistical precision, a survey cannot be considered scientific, at least not for the purposes of making estimates on the prevalence of some variable of interest.

A lack of external validity typically results when poorly planned mail surveys and call-in telephone polling are used, for example, to measure voting intentions or attitudes toward social issues. A striking example of this occurred while the original edition of this book was being written in 1984. A prominent radio station in Chicago sponsored a call-in telephone poll to determine whether more persons backed Chicago's mayor or his city council opponents. Nearly 30,000 calls were made to one of two "900" telephone numbers to register preference. Seventy-five percent of these calls supported the mayor's opponents. A few weeks later the Northwestern University Survey Laboratory conducted an RDD telephone survey (i.e., a probability sampling technique) and scientifically determined that about 40% of Chicago residents supported the mayor, only 20% backed his opponents, and the remainder sided with neither faction. These scientific results were very different from the uncontrolled and thus unreliable (i.e., inaccurate), nonprobability "sampling method" used by the radio station. (By the way, the mayor won the next general election with nearly a 60% majority vote.)

Estimating Multivariate Relationships

If a survey is not intended to estimate the level at which a variable exists in the population but rather to study interrelationships *among* variables, true probability sampling may be less important. For example, in the case of someone interested in measuring the correlation between fear of crime, age, race, and gender, a sampling design that ensures a heterogeneous sample, but not necessarily a random one, may well suffice. Here the purpose of the survey would be to estimate not the proportion of the population who were fearful, but rather what types of people were most or least fearful. Nonprobability sampling schemes may be adequate for these needs.

Evaluation Research

A third purpose for which a survey may be needed is that of evaluation research (see Weiss, 1972). For example, if an evaluator conducted a panel study (a survey in which the same respondents were interviewed at two or more points in time) to determine the effect of a local antiharassment public service campaign on employees' experience with sexual harassment, it may not be necessary to draw a probability sample of the population of interest at Wave 1, since it is *change* in the prevalence of harassment that is being investigated (cf. Lavrakas & Tyler, 1983). This reasoning assumes that the variable of interest is not confounded (i.e., correlated) with the types of persons who are sampled—which is a plausible assumption in many instances.

Summary

The purpose of the survey, then, will determine whether a probability sample is required or whether a nonprobability sample is adequate. Then, assuming it is decided to conduct a telephone survey, a decision can be made whether to employ some form of RDD or whether an existing list can be used from which to draw the sample. If the purpose is to estimate a population parameter in the general population, then RDD will almost always be the sampling method of choice. On the other hand, if a telephone survey is meant to estimate a population parameter of some small subset of the general population (e.g., all members of the American Medical Association), then random/systematic list sampling would certainly be preferable.

Who Will Be Sampled?

The practical matter of who will be interviewed may also influence the choice of sampling design, especially from a cost standpoint. If a survey must sample some small subset of the general population, then often a list exists that will provide an adequate sampling frame. For example, if male nurses constitute the population of interest, then representative lists of nurses need to be gathered from which to create the sampling pool, with gender being screened once contact is made through the survey's introduction. In contrast, if working women in the general population define the set of eligible respondents, then an RDD survey that subsequently screens for employed females would be the most practical and cost-effective method of choice, since as many as one half of all households are likely to contain an eligible respondent.

Serious problems can arise when telephone sampling must be restricted to relatively small geographic boundaries, such as when sampling only in certain neighborhoods. In this instance RDD sampling may not be cost-acceptable because interviewers would be likely to reach an extremely large proportion of ineligible households because telephone prefixes rarely conform to neighborhood boundaries. Furthermore, it is often difficult for citizens to accurately identify themselves as living within or outside of a survey's geographic boundaries. In this case, if the survey's purpose is to estimate neighborhood-level parameters, then a telephone survey may not work. In contrast, if it can be reasoned that one need not be concerned about missing residents who live in households with unlisted telephone numbers, then the use of a reverse telephone directory (i.e., a special directory that orders names and telephone numbers by street address) should solve the problem. Unfortunately, this will never be the preferred approach when one wants to gather data with high external validity.

Prevalence of Missing Numbers

Assuming that sampling will be done of the public at large and the purpose of the survey is to estimate population parameters, then the proportion of households with unlisted telephone numbers and the residential mobility within the sampling area can influence the decision of whether to use some form of RDD or to draw a probability sample from a directory or other listing. Experience shows that surveys designed to gather valid estimates of population parameters in large cities will almost always require RDD, given that as many as half of all residential telephone numbers will not be published in the current directory (see Survey Sampling, Inc., 1990). In smaller cities and suburbs the proportion of telephone numbers that are missing from the local directory decreases, whereas in some rural areas it may be so low as to eliminate the need to employ RDD.

To make an informed decision about directory sampling versus RDD, one needs to know the approximate proportion of households whose numbers are not published. Sometimes local telephone companies will provide this information, but often they will not. In the latter instance a surveyor needs to estimate this proportion. One approach to estimation is to determine the approximate number of residential telephone numbers in the local directory, adjust it for multiple household listings, and compare it to census statistics on the number of households in the sampling area. Although there are no accepted standards here, I would recommend against directory sampling if the proportion of missing numbers is estimated to be greater than 10%-15%. Again, the reader is reminded that this problem is usually not an issue unless the survey's purpose is to estimate the level at which a variable exists in the general population.

Availability of Resources

A final consideration, but not necessarily the least important, is the amount of resources (including paid and unpaid person-time) available for generating sampling pools and for interviewing. Both list sampling and

RDD sampling pools can be generated by hand or by computer. The size of the sampling pool that needs to be generated and the size of the final sample that will be interviewed need to be considered. For example, if 2,000 respondents will be interviewed and the purpose of the survey is to study the interrelationships of variables and not to estimate univariate population parameters, then a computer-generated RDD sampling pool may still be preferred over a hand-drawn directory sample, from the standpoint of the reduced person-time it would take to generate the sampling pool using a computer versus doing it manually. On the other hand, if only 15% of a target population is missing from a recent telephone directory and rough estimates of population values are acceptable, then directory sampling may be the preferred choice for a surveyor who cannot afford the additional interviewing time that likely would be needed with RDD.

A practical consideration that directly affects the choice of method that will be used to generate a sampling pool is the trade-off between the cost of generating the sampling pool and the cost of interviewing. If, for example, relatively inexpensive work-study students are available to gather detailed telephone information to help a researcher create a highly efficient sampling pool, then total survey costs might be reduced considerably by minimizing the time higher priced interviewers dialed unproductive numbers. In contrast, if interviewing is relatively inexpensive whereas it would be very expensive to create a highly efficient sampling pool, one might opt for a relatively easily generated sampling pool that interviewers "cleaned" via dialing.

Each decision on what type of sampling should be done for a survey is an important one. It is definitely not an arbitrary one and often requires compromises, that is, the "creative tension" in survey planning that Henry (1990) discusses. These trade-offs may require sacrificing some degree of precision for the purposes of feasibility. The extent to which one can sacrifice precision and still gather useful (i.e., essentially valid) data is certainly debatable. Whatever is decided, the surveyor must be able to defend the sampling decisions.

RANDOM DIGIT DIALING (RDD)

First proposed by Cooper (1964), random digit dialing (RDD) is a group of probability sampling techniques that provides a nonzero chance of reaching any household within a sampling area that has a telephone access line (i.e., a unique telephone number that rings in that household only) regardless of whether its telephone number is published or listed. RDD does not provide an *equal* probability of reaching every telephone household in a sampling area because some households have more than one telephone access line. For households with two or more telephone lines postsampling adjustments (weighting) are often made before the data are analyzed to correct for this unequal probability of selection. The need for such adjustments will depend on the survey's purpose.

A fairly sizable proportion of the American public, though not yet a majority, has unpublished (not printed in a local telephone directory, but accessible through directory information) or unlisted (not accessible at all) telephone numbers. Recent estimates suggest that about one in three household telephone numbers is unlisted (Survey Sampling, Inc., 1990). This proportion has been growing slightly each year and for psychological reasons can be expected to continue to increase, especially in urban areas where those most likely to have unlisted telephone numbers typically live. Despite the often-held assumption that most of those who do not list their telephone numbers live in higher income, white households, it is lower income, minority Americans who, as a group, are most likely to have unlisted telephone numbers.

A general rule is that the farther one samples from central cities the lower the proportion of households with unlisted telephone numbers. Thus, inner-ring suburbs typically will have a lower proportion of unlisted telephone numbers than their central city. Outer-ring suburbs will have even lower levels, and as one moves into rural areas the "unlisted phenomenon" often dwindles. For example, nearly 50% of all City of Chicago households have unlisted numbers; in inner-ring suburbs of Chicago such as Evanston, this drops to about 25%-35%. As one moves further away from Chicago city limits, outer-ring suburbs show a 20%-25% unlisted rate. In essentially rural areas outside the suburbs it often drops to as low as 10%.

Unlisted telephone numbers are a potential barrier to representative sampling when a survey's purpose is to estimate the level at which certain variables exist in the general population. The unlisted problem would be likely to increase a survey's noncoverage error because it is not a random subset of the general population that chooses not to list telephone numbers. As mentioned earlier, income is generally inversely related to non-listing. Also, women, single adults, and those with relatively less education are more likely not to list their telephone numbers. Not surprisingly, higher fear of crime is directly related to having an unlisted telephone number (Lavrakas et al., 1980). Also, nonresponse rates have been found to be slightly higher for households with unlisted numbers (Drew, Choudhry, & Hunter, 1988).

RDD reduces the potential problem of noncoverage error caused by unlisted telephone numbers. Once a surveyor knows the prefixes (i.e., the first three digits in a local telephone number) that ring within the sampling boundaries, various techniques can be used to add random digit suffixes to produce seven-digit local telephone numbers that may or may not be working, and if working, may or may not ring in households *regardless whether the number is listed*. (For telephone surveys that cross area codes, ten-digit numbers must be used.)

When it has been decided that some form of RDD sampling will take place, the pool of numbers that will be processed by interviewers can be generated by hand or by computer. It is almost always preferable to do this by computer, but it is not necessary to do so. Theoretically, any approach to generating RDD sampling pools by computer can be done manually. In practice, however, it is often much too time-consuming to justify the manual approach.

Getting Ready for Generating
Most RDD Sampling Pools

One practical advantage of RDD is that it does not require a fully delineated sampling frame from which to draw the sampling pool; that is, one does not need to have a listing of all possible telephone numbers in a sampling area. Conveniently, RDD replicates exactly what would occur if one were to have a complete sampling frame of all possible numbers, but does so with considerably less effort. With the chance that any telephone number that rings within the sampling boundaries will be generated, the sampling pool that RDD creates replicates that which would result if one were to create a fully delineated sampling frame.

Gathering Telephone Prefixes

The first step in generating a sampling pool for most RDD techniques is to assemble an exhaustive list of prefixes that ring within the geographic boundaries of the sampling area. This is often not a straightforward or easy task. Sometimes the boundaries of the sampling area and the boundaries of the prefixes that ring in the sampling area coincide exactly. Other times, boundaries of telephone prefixes coincide somewhat closely with the geographic perimeter of the desired sampling area. In still other cases the prefix boundaries do not closely approximate the sampling area's boundaries. In this latter instance RDD sampling may have to be ruled out as too costly, which in turn may negate the value of the survey. In the case in which prefix boundaries are fairly close to the boundaries of the preferred sampling area, it may be possible to use geographic screening questions to exclude those who live outside the sampling area, or, instead, one may choose to shrink or expand the sampling area to conform to the perimeter defined by the prefixes. As always, these are not arbitrary decisions and it remains the responsibility of the surveyor to determine the extent to which the survey's purpose might be compromised by such trade-offs.

Those planning a national, state, or regional (within an entire area code or several area codes) RDD telephone survey are advised to use a current diskette (or tape) of AT&T's data base of all the area codes and prefixes that are activated in the United States and surrounding nations. In 1992 this data base could be purchased from Bellcore (Morristown, New Jersey) for approximately $400 and contained approximately 50,000 area code and prefix combinations, although not all of these are used for residential access lines.

For those planning RDD surveys that do not cover entire area codes, (e.g., a survey of 10 contiguous suburbs, or three counties, etc.), prefix information often must be gathered manually. The assistance one can expect from local telephone companies in providing information about telephone prefixes will vary. The easiest approach is knowing someone who works for the telephone company who will provide the prefix information you seek. Apart from this, an individual's own creative persever- ance will often yield prefix information from the telephone company that a less persistent researcher will not obtain.

If the telephone company chooses not to help, all is not lost. By using a reverse directory or even a regular telephone directory one can gather fairly reliable estimates of the information originally sought from the tele- phone company. Using a reverse directory is easier, because the expressed purpose of such volumes is to list telephone numbers in geographic order. Furthermore, some reverse directories also provide useful aggregate sta- tistics, such as the number of listed residential accounts associate with each prefix.

When a reverse directory is not available the task is more time-consuming and sometimes simply not feasible. By assembling all the local telephone directories that serve the sampling area, a surveyor can methodically determine the match between prefixes and the perimeter of the sampling area. This is done using a map to systematically plot the location of prefixes based on the addresses found in the telephone directories. De- pending upon the size of one's sampling area, this can be an extremely time-consuming process. In fact, for anything but a relatively small local area, this approach is often impractical.

Determining the Number of Lines per Prefix

As will be discussed later in greater detail, it is also useful to know the number of residential telephone access lines in operation for each prefix in the sampling area. Providing it is uniformly accurate for each prefix, this information can be used to generate random telephone numbers in the proportion that each prefix exists within the sampling area; in this way, the final sampling pool will be *stratified* by prefix. Ideally this information can be retrieved from the telephone companies servicing the sampling area. But even if one has to rely on telephone directories for these data, it is possible to systematically sample prefixes from a representative sample of pages within directories to estimate the relative proportion of residential telephone lines associated with the various prefixes that will be used. (This latter approach assumes that the proportion of unlisted telephone numbers is fairly constant across prefixes. If this assumption cannot be made, this approach should not be used.)

For example, in the city of Evanston, Illinois, there are eight residential prefixes. By sampling telephone numbers from pages in the Evanston directory one would learn that three of these prefixes are used for nearly two thirds of all residential access lines. When generating an RDD sampling pool for Evanston, it is most efficient (from the standpoint of interviewer processing time) to do so in a manner that reflects this distribution of prefixes. This approach is quite feasible when sampling is confined to relatively small geographical areas.

Identifying Nonworking Banks of Suffixes

Information about vacuous banks of suffixes (numerical ranges of telephone numbers that do not operate or that contain no residential access lines) can also be used to improve the efficiency of an RDD sampling pool. If this type of information is not readily forthcoming from the telephone company, a reverse directory can be used. By closely scanning the numerically ordered listing of each prefix one can find ranges of vacuous suffixes. The validity of this method hinges on the fact that telephone companies do not assign unlisted telephone numbers from special banks of suffixes. Instead, an available telephone number is first assigned to a new customer, and then the company asks the customer whether he or she wants the number published or listed. Thus by "eyeballing" the numerically ordered listing of telephone numbers in a reverse directory, one can methodically determine which banks of suffixes are operational. I recommend that the metric used in this search be in ranges of 100—that is, the surveyor should determine whether numbers exist in the 0000-0099 bank of suffixes, the 0100-0199 bank, the 0200-0299 bank, and so on for each prefix.

This can be an onerous task when the sampling area contains hundreds of prefixes, but using such information will significantly reduce the proportion of nonworking numbers in RDD sampling, which in turn reduces the time and cost of interviewing. If a reverse directory is unavailable, this information can also be estimated from regular telephone directories, but this is an extremely time-consuming task. It remains the decision of each surveyor whether or not to gather such information about each prefix. If, for example, low cost or "free" (i.e., no direct cost) student-time is available to work on assembling such information, but a researcher will have to pay for interviewers' time, then it may be well worth the effort to improve the efficiency of the sampling pool by gathering such information.

If one intends to conduct RDD sampling of the same geographic area in several studies (i.e., year after year), then it is often worth the initial costs to gather as much information as possible about the prefixes in that area. Depending on residential mobility in the sampling area, it is important to periodically update (e.g., annually) both information about the proportion of households assigned to each prefix and information about ranges of nonoperating banks of suffixes.

Simple RDD Sampling Versus
Multistage RDD Sampling

As will be discussed later in more detail, there are situations in which a researcher may have information only about which prefixes ring in the sampling area or may choose to not gather any other information. In this case, one of two approaches can be used. The first is simple RDD sampling, whereby random digits are added to the prefixes, prefixes are used in equal numbers, and interviewers' time is used to clean the unproductive numbers (e.g., those that do not reach households in a survey of the general public) from the sampling pool. In the second case, the sampling pool is most commonly generated in a two-stage fashion. In the first stage, a relatively small number of telephone numbers are generated using the simple RDD approach. These numbers are called and those that reach households are used to generate the full sampling pool in the second stage.

Exactly how this two-stage approach is accomplished is explained later, but the issue is raised here because the decision a researcher faces about how much information to try to gather for use in generating the sampling pool is heavily dependent upon the costs associated with gathering this information versus interviewing costs. If interviewers' time is expensive relative to the cost of generating the sampling pool, then it behooves the researcher to create the most efficient sampling pool possible. If the reverse were the case, then the researcher should opt for an easily generated, but not necessarily efficient, sampling pool and let "low-priced" interviewers (e.g., unpaid students) clean it by dialing a large proportion of unproductive numbers. (A further consideration is that the two-stage approach has larger sampling error relative to the simple RDD approach.)

Hand-Generated RDD Sampling Pools

Although rarely used, it is instructive to begin by looking at the manual approach to producing a pool of RDD telephone numbers. This sequencing has been chosen because the manual approach is a methodical and simplified version of what the computer can do more quickly and efficiently, and so should be more easily understood by those readers new to this part of telephone survey methodology.

There are two basic techniques that can be used to generate RDD sampling pools by hand. First, one can use a random numbers table (found in the back of most statistics books) to choose strings of consecutive digits to serve as suffixes to add to three-digit prefixes that ring in the sampling area. Second, one can use an *added-digit(s)* technique with telephone numbers sampled directly from telephone directories, although in strict terms this latter approach may not meet the requirement of providing every possible telephone number in a sampling area a nonzero chance of selection.

Using a Random Numbers Table

The first example will illustrate the simplest case of RDD sampling pool generation, in which the only information known to the surveyor is the prefixes that ring in the sampling area. Once this list of prefixes has been assembled, one simply adds consecutive strings of four digits from the random numbers table to each prefix, one at a time. Suppose one finds the following string of random digits: 547196353826. For the purpose of this example, also suppose there were only three prefixes in the sampling area: 864, 866, and 869. Then the first three telephone numbers formed would be 864-5471, 866-9635, and 869-3826. The person creating the sampling pool would continue this process until a sufficient number of telephone numbers have been generated. (How to estimate what is likely to be a sufficiently large sampling pool is discussed later in this chapter.)

If the surveyor also has complete and accurate information about the relative proportion of telephone access lines within the sampling area reached by each prefix, then that information could be used to reduce subsequent interviewer processing time. With the above set of three prefixes, suppose that 864 reached 20% of the households in the sampling area, while 866 and 869 each reached 40%, respectively. Then the person generating the sampling pool from a random numbers table should add strings of four digits to prefixes chosen in the following order: 864, 866, 866, 869, 869, 864, 866, 866, 869, 869, and so on, to reflect the proportional distribution of prefixes in the sampling area (i.e., 2:4:4).

If accurate and complete information is also known about the ranges of nonoperating (i.e., vacuous) banks of suffixes, this too can be used to improve the efficiency of a sampling pool of RDD numbers in reaching working telephones. Again, using the same set of three prefixes from the previous examples, assume the 864 prefix only operates with suffixes that range from 2000 to 3999, the 866 prefix works from 5000-7999, and 869 works from 0000-0999 and from 4000-4999. The person who is generating the sampling pool should then chose strings of only three digits in length from the random numbers table. Three random digits would then be added to the following prefixes and the known-to-be-operating leading suffix digit: 864-2, 864-3, 866-5, 866-6, 866-7, 869-0, and 869-4. Sudman (1973) refers to this process as the *inverse sampling method*.

It should be noted that regardless of the method used to generate an RDD sampling pool, information about prefixes is properly used only when it is available for all prefixes in the sampling pool and uniformly accurate across all prefixes. The reason for this is that without equally accurate information about all prefixes the surveyor will not be able to accurately calculate the relative proportion of numbers that need to be generated for each prefix. Proper use of this additional information also assumes that the proportion of numbers per prefix that are unlisted is relatively equal, which is a reasonable assumption in many sampling areas. In those cases in which even one of these criteria is not met it is best to use the simple RDD approach (or the two-stage method described later) and leave it to the interviewers' processing of numbers to achieve the proper sampling of prefixes.

This proper sampling happens because of the self-weighting aspect of RDD surveys. That is, interviews will theoretically be completed at prefixes at a rate directly proportional to the relative frequency of those prefixes in the sampling area. When one has comparable information about all prefixes in the sampling area, the efficiency of this self-weighting process can be enhanced. If comparable information does not exist, the rule to follow is, "Let well enough alone!" This caveat also holds for information about vacuous banks of suffixes. Unless complete suffix information has been gathered about all prefixes in the sampling area and unless the proportion of unlisted numbers is relatively uniform across prefixes, it is best to employ the straightforward approach of simply using prefixes in equal proportions and adding random digits to each.

An additional comment that holds for all RDD sampling: It is possible to combine the efficiency gained from knowing both the proportion of working numbers associated with each prefix and the information about vacuous banks of suffixes associated with each prefix. This is rather complicated to do by hand, but it is possible, and if there are not too many prefixes it justifies the time and attentiveness it will demand.

Added-Digit(s) Techniques

Landon and Banks (1977) provided an empirical test of the efficiency of this approach to generating telephone sampling pools. This general technique samples "seed" numbers from a telephone directory, adds a fixed or random digit (or two or three) to the suffix of each seed, and uses these new numbers in the sampling pool. The new numbers that are produced via this approach may be listed or unlisted ones. Lepkowski (1988) observes that, "to establish that unlisted numbers have a nonzero chance of being selected, it must be assumed that unlisted numbers are evenly mixed among listed numbers" (p. 93). Lepkowski believes that this is "an unlikely assumption." Although I am not in close agreement with his view, I second Lepkowski's caution that despite these techniques being relatively simple to apply, there are uncertainties about the selection probabilities of the individual numbers that are generated. This concern notwithstanding, a situation may result in which a surveyor is forced to make a choice between feasibility/timing and the possibility of somewhat increasing total survey error. As is noted throughout this book, these are among the many practical decisions (trade-offs) that surveyors constantly face.

The way in which digits are added can vary. For example, the "plus-one" approach can be used. In this case a number, such as 869-5025, is randomly or systematically chosen from a telephone directory that covers the sampling area. A 1 is added to the last digit of the suffix producing the number 869-5026, which in turn enters the sampling pool. Another approach would be to add 11 (thereby yielding 869-5036) or a one-digit or two-digit random number to each seed sampled from the directory.

These approaches to sample generation are especially useful when one must quickly generate a relatively small sampling pool by hand; for example, one that might require upwards of 1,000 telephone numbers. The approach also helps the survey process by shortening the interviewing period, as it increases the proportion of working numbers that will be dialed compared to simple RDD sampling. In two studies reported by Landon and Banks (1977) the add-a-digit approach improved sampling efficiency by approximately 30%. The effect is similar to the aforementioned technique whereby information about nonoperating banks of suffixes is used to target the generation of telephone numbers within working banks of suffixes.

To use an added-digit(s) approach one must first gather a comprehensive set of telephone directories and then determine the number of seeds that should be drawn from each book. In the simplest case there will be one directory. After estimating the size of the sampling pool that will be needed to achieve the desired sample size of completed interviews, the surveyor should compare this amount with the total number of telephone numbers listed in the directory or directories and choose seeds either randomly or systematically on pages throughout the directory.

Landon and Banks (1977) caution about possible bias in add-a-digit sampling that could result if telephone companies concentrate the assignment of unlisted telephone numbers to certain banks of suffixes (see Lepkowski, 1988). If this were to happen, the sample of telephone numbers based on the seeds listed in the directory might cause considerable coverage error. In other words, the pool of numbers that was dialed may be biased against those who have unlisted telephone numbers. Despite this concern, I am unaware of any telephone company where this is the actual practice followed in assigning unlisted numbers; rather a number is first assigned and then it is the customer who indicates whether it is to be listed, unpublished, or unlisted. Nevertheless, to be safe, it is prudent that anyone planning to employ an added-digit(s) approach first determine local telephone companies' practices associated with unlisted numbers.

If a surveyor plans to use a telephone survey on a one-shot basis (e.g., for a master's thesis) and is uncertain whether this method of data collection will be employed in the foreseeable future, then the manual approach to generating a pool of RDD numbers will probably be the preferred choice, providing the size of the pool is not extremely large (several thousand). However, if the size of the pool of numbers that must be processed is very large or if a surveyor expects to be regularly using telephone surveys to gather data within the same sampling area, it is strongly recommended that RDD sampling pools be generated by computer.

Computer-Generated RDD Sampling Pools

Each of the techniques for generating RDD samples discussed above has its counterpart when using a computer to generate the sampling pool. When one has CATI, the steps taken to generate RDD samples may be quite different than the realities facing surveyors without CATI. With some CATI systems, telephone numbers can be generated for use by interviewers one at a time, as they are needed; thus, it may not be necessary to generate the sampling pool in advance with CATI. In contrast, persons without CATI will need a sufficiently large sampling pool of RDD numbers waiting for interviewers in advance of interviewing sessions, as it would be impractical to have someone at the interviewing sessions generating RDD numbers one at a time as interviewers needed them.

As with all RDD sampling pool generation, the use of a computer begins with the collection of an exhaustive list of all prefixes that ring within the sampling boundaries. As previously discussed, it can be quite cost-effective to gather additional information about each prefix: specifically, (a) the number of residential accounts associated with each prefix and (b) ranges of vacuous suffix banks for each prefix. An important reminder: Unless additional information is uniformly accurate and available for *all prefixes* used in sampling, it should not be used!

Thus with the possibility of three types of prefix information available, there are four situations a surveyor will encounter:

1. having the list of prefixes, only;
2. having the list of prefixes and information about the number of residential accounts on each prefix;
3. having the list of prefixes and ranges of vacuous suffixes for each prefix; and
4. having all three types of information.

Prefixes Only

The simplest case is when the surveyor has only the list of prefixes that ring in the sampling area. In this instance a computer is programmed to assign an equal number of random suffixes to each prefix, until a sufficiently large pool of numbers has been generated. If, for example, one has an estimated need for a sampling pool with 1,000 RDD numbers and there are 10 prefixes in the sampling area, then simple division indicates that each prefix should be paired with 100 unique strings of four-digit random numbers. Depending upon the speed of the printer used, the following BASIC program, for example, would generate and print 1,000 numbers (100 for each of the 10 prefixes listed in the DATA statements), in a few minutes on a DOS-PC:

```
5   RANDOMIZE TIMER
10  FOR I=1 TO 10
20      READ PREFIX(I)
30      FOR X=1 TO 100
40          SUFF1=INT(RND*9)
50          SUFF2=INT(RND*9)
60          SUFF3=INT(RND*9)
70          SUFF4=INT(RND*9)
80          LPRINT PREFIX(I);"-";SUFF1;SUFF2;SUFF3;SUFF4
90      NEXT X
100 NEXT I
110 DATA 251,256,328,475,491,492,570,864,866,869
```

Or, this program could be amended to produce an ASCII file for printing at a later time.

With use of a computer (or even a random numbers table) to generate random digit strings, there is a small probability that duplicate strings will be generated and matched with the same prefix. In other words, if the suffix string 4567 were generated and paired with two different prefixes (e.g., 251-4567 and 869-4567), there would be no problem. But occasionally the exact same telephone number will appear again, by chance. In the case of hand-generated samples, it could be impractical to check for duplicates. However, computers can easily check for duplicates, and it is often worth incorporating such a routine into the program (e.g., in SPSS, a widely available statistical software package, the "lag" command can be used to identify duplicates; see LeBailly & Lavrakas, 1981).

In addition to cleaning the sampling pool for duplicates, one may choose to program the computer to perform other cleaning procedures, such as eliminating all numbers that end in 00 and/or 000 and/or 0000. These numbers are typically nonresidential; thus eliminating them can save on interviewer processing time without necessarily compromising the validity of the sampling pool (i.e., without increasing noncoverage error). This should be done with caution and only after checking a reverse directory to determine the validity of this assumption. Because businesses, by their very nature, list their telephone numbers, a fairly quick check of a reverse directory will indicate whether telephone numbers that end in multiple zeros are almost all business numbers. If not, then such a cleaning routine should not be used as it needlessly could add to noncoverage error.

Nonworking Banks of Suffixes

When banks of nonoperating suffixes have been identified, this information can also be incorporated into the computer routine. This can be done in two ways. First, as mentioned earlier, if banks of suffixes in ranges of 1,000 can be identified as nonoperating (e.g., 1000-1999 or 3000-3999), then the computer can be programmed to utilize such information. A second approach is to have four-digit numbers (i.e., the three digits of the prefix and the leading digit of the suffix) read as data and program the computer to generate random strings of three digits in length. Using an earlier example, suppose there are three prefixes in the sampling area and each has a relatively narrow range of operating suffixes: 864-2000 through 864-3999; 866-5000 through 866-7999; 869-0000 through 869-0999; and 869-4000 through 869-4999. In this case the following four-digit strings should be read as data: 8642, 8643, 8665, 8666, 8667, 8690, and 8694. The computer would be programmed to add strings of three random digits. This would generate a pool of RDD numbers concentrated (stratified) only in those banks of suffixes known to contain working residential telephones.

Number of Access Lines

Finally, if a surveyor knows the number of telephone access lines associated with each prefix, the sampling pool of RDD numbers can be stratified by prefix. Again, for the sake of simplicity assume that information about vacuous suffixes is not known. If it were determined that the 864 prefix had 4,000 working numbers, 866 had 3,000, and 869 had 1,000, one would start by calculating the relative frequency (proportion) of each prefix in the sampling area. Of the 8,000 total access lines, 50% are reached via 864, 37.5% via 866, and 12.5% via 869. Thus, if a researcher estimated that interviewers would need to process 1,000 RDD numbers, then the sampling pool should contain 500 with the 864 prefix, 375 with 866, and 125 with 869.

To accomplish this with a DOS-PC, for example, the BASIC program presented earlier would be modified as follows:

```
  5  RANDOMIZE TIMER
 10  FOR I=1 TO 3
 20     READ PREFIX(I)
 25     READ NUMB(I)
 30     FOR X=1 TO NUMB(I)
 40        SUFF1=INT(RND*9)
 50        SUFF2=INT(RND*9)
 60        SUFF3=INT(RND*9)
 70        SUFF4=INT(RND*9)
 80        LPRINT PREFIX(I);"-";SUFF1;SUFF2;SUFF3;SUFF4
 90     NEXT X
100  NEXT I
110  DATA 864,500,866,375,869,125
```

If information also was known about vacuous suffix banks for each prefix, it too could be incorporated into the program, although, as before, adjustments would need to be programmed into the routine to reflect the proper proportion of the final sampling pool associated with each prefix.

Multistage RDD Sampling Pools

Mitofsky (1970) and Waksberg (1978) pioneered a somewhat complex approach to RDD sampling that is often used by large survey organizations because of its practical value in generating highly efficient large sampling pools and its potential for considerable reduction of interviewing costs versus a small increase in sampling error. In its typical form this approach has two stages: Stage 1 uses simple RDD to identify a relatively small number of household telephone numbers (typically 50-100) within the sampling area that are then used as seeds (or clusters) in Stage 2. This approach is especially attractive when the sampling area is so large as to discourage one from assembling exhaustive information about prefixes, other than a complete listing (e.g., national, regional, or statewide surveys).

The convenience and efficiency of this approach has its trade-off in somewhat increasing the survey's sampling error (see discussion of design effects in Kish, 1965; Groves, 1989; Lepkowski, 1988; Henry, 1990). In evaluating this trade-off, Groves observes, "despite the loss of precision for survey statistics from cluster samples, every major U.S. federal government household survey and almost all academic and commercial household surveys use cluster designs" (p. 260).

Using an example of a national survey will help to illustrate the two-stage RDD approach to creating a sampling pool. A surveyor would begin by securing a listing of all residential telephone prefixes that cover the nation; this is most easily done by purchasing Bellcore's computerized data base of all area codes and prefixes (at a cost of approximately $400 in 1992). As of the early 1990s, of all possible RDD numbers that can be generated for the United States approximately one in four will reach a household. Based on advice from someone with expertise in sampling statistics, a presampling decision should be made on how many clusters (the unique household numbers identified at Stage 1) will be used in the sampling design; typically this number is in the 50-100 range. Stage 1 would then require the generation of a preliminary sampling pool of a size approximately four times the number of clusters that will be used. For a researcher using the Bellcore data base and planning a survey with a final sample size of 1,100 using 100 Stage 1 clusters, the process at Stage 1 would require randomly selecting 400 (100 × 4) area code/prefix combinations from the approximately 50,000 combinations in the Bellcore data base. Then random four-digit suffixes would be added to each to create 400 ten-digit telephone numbers.

Interviewers would then dial these 400 numbers to determine which reached households, expecting about 100 of them to do so. This is rarely a straightforward process and the surveyor should become familiar with the literature before having interviewers begin any dialing (see, for example, Alexander, 1988; Burkheimer & Levinsohn, 1988; Mason & Immerman, 1988). In some cases, interviewers might simply complete a short "screener" questionnaire to verify the household status of the numbers that are answered; in other cases, a researcher may have actual full-length interviews completed with each household reached. Regardless, *all* numbers used in Stage 1 must be categorized as being a household (including refusals and residential answering machines) or not. This cannot always be accomplished via interviewing and research staff will need to devote time and expense to contacting local telephone companies to try to determine whether numbers that are never answered are households. (For example, a two-stage national RDD survey conducted by NUSL in 1992 required approximately 3% of the Stage 1 numbers to be resolved through contact with local telephone companies despite interviewers calling these numbers more than 20 times each. Stage 1 of this survey took over two weeks to resolve the status of every number in the sampling pool.)

For a national survey the household numbers identified at Stage 1 represent a simple random sample of all telephone households in the nation. In the present example, with a final sample size of 1,100 planned, 11 Stage 2 interviews would be completed at each of the 100 Stage 1 clusters. This is accomplished by taking each Stage 1 household number and randomly replacing the last two digits of the suffix (at least 11 times). This is done for each cluster until the desired number of completions is attained. Because at least 11 Stage 2 numbers will be needed for each cluster, 1,100 unique numbers can be generated to begin the Stage 2 sampling pool. Past experience indicates that as many as 60% of these Stage 2 numbers will reach households (Lepkowski, 1988). Comparing this to the 25% household "hit-rate" in Stage 1 demonstrates the strong appeal of this approach from the standpoint of reducing interviewer processing time; that is, Stage 2 is more than twice as efficient as Stage 1 in reaching households. In Stage 2 for each number that does not lead to a completion a new number in that cluster is generated to replace it.

In practice, generating the Stage 2 sampling pool is complicated and best managed with a computer data base that is constantly updated. Furthermore, not all clusters will yield the desired number of completions, although unequal numbers of completions per cluster can be adjusted through postsampling weighting (see Lepkowski, 1988). Readers who intend to use multistage RDD sampling are encouraged to become very familiar with its many practical and statistical nuances through additional reading (e.g., Groves et al., 1988; Potthoff, 1987) and discussing one's own particular application with someone else with extensive practical experience with the approach.

DIRECTORY AND LIST-BASED
SAMPLING POOLS

Depending on the purpose of the survey, there are many instances in which RDD is unnecessary to meet a surveyor's needs. The reader is reminded that RDD is the preferred method to avoid noncoverage error in selecting a representative sample of households (with telephones) from the general population. But when an accurate listing of a population of interest is available, then sampling usually should be done from this list-based sampling frame.

The problem, however, is that accurate lists often are not available to the interested surveyor. Frey (1989) discusses several problems associated with list sampling for telephone surveys. These include restricted access, ineligible listings, duplicate listings, and incorrect and omitted listings. For example, given that nearly one in five U.S. households move each year, many lists will have outdated residential telephone numbers.

An example of creating a sampling pool from a list would be a telephone survey of members of a professional organization (e.g., retired military officers), in which the organization has a complete listing of each member's home and/or business telephone number; this listing would serve as the sampling frame for this survey. Another example of list sampling would be a telephone survey of students presently enrolled at a university, in which a list from the registrar's office (the sampling frame) would define the entire population of interest. As mentioned before, in some rural areas of the United States relatively few persons have unlisted telephone numbers and there often is a very low rate of population ingress. In areas such as this, the local telephone directory may be used to pick numbers for the sampling pool, but concern for noncoverage error should always guide the researcher's choice.

Forming a sampling pool via list sampling is uncomplicated and can be done randomly or systematically. The random approach, however, is rarely necessary provided one samples in a systematic fashion throughout an entire listing. Still, some persons may prefer to choose the random approach, and thus a brief illustration is appropriate.

Random Approach

Suppose that a telephone survey of 200 school teachers' satisfaction with working conditions was to be conducted for a school district that employed 1,800 teachers. In the easiest case the district's computer could be programmed to randomly choose 200 (or more) names for the sampling pool. (The reader is reminded that in almost all telephone surveys the sampling pool will need to be larger than the final sample size desired, due in part to the problem of nonresponse. But for this example, we will assume that all teachers who are chosen for the sampling pool will be reached and will participate in the survey.) If there were no computer to generate this sample, it could be done by hand in a variety of ways, using a random numbers table. One way would be to use two-digit strings of random numbers to "count forward" to the next name on a complete alphabetical listing of all 1,800 teachers. For example, if the random numbers table showed the following string, 0417565439, then the fourth teacher on an alphabetical listing would be the first one to enter the sampling pool. Next the person generating the sample would count ahead 17 names to choose the second teacher; then ahead 56 names for the third; and so on. Using this approach to sampling 200 names from the listing of 1,800 would require the person generating the sampling pool to go back through the list approximately five or six times. This follows from the fact that, by chance, one pass through the list would sample an average of 36 names, which in turn projects the need to go through the list about 5.5 times to get the 200 names.

Systematic Approach

A much easier and typically the preferred approach from the standpoint of reduced sampling error is systematic sampling from a list (see Henry, 1990). Take the same example in which the school district wanted to interview 200 teachers from a staff of 1,800; thus, one ninth of the staff should be sampled. First, a random number from 1 through 9 would be chosen and that many names would be counted from the start of the alphabetical listing to sample the first teacher. After that, every ninth name on the list would be chosen. If the random start is the number 2, then the second teacher on the list would be the first name to enter the sampling pool. After that, the pool would include the 11th, 20th, 29th, 38th, and so on name on the list.

When sampling from a very long list, such as a local telephone book, it is much easier not to count ahead to names, one at a time; rather, the following example illustrates a technique that accomplishes the same systematic sampling more quickly. Assume that a sampling pool of 300 residential telephone numbers was to be drawn from a directory. Also assume that the directory had 50 pages, with four columns of numbers on each page. One should sample six numbers per page ($300 \div 50 = 6$). Because there are four columns per page, one could choose some arbitrary (i.e., unbiased) scheme for sampling within columns. The possibilities are infinite. For example, one could sample the 10th residential listing from the top in each of the four columns and the fifth from the bottom in the first two columns, thus yielding a total of six names per page. To reduce the tedium further, one might construct a template to place over each page or draw a cluster sample, although the latter increases sampling error (see Lepkowski, 1988, pp. 76-78).

With list sampling, it is important to remember to employ a technique that chooses names *throughout* the entire listing. Since lists are typically alphabetized, this results in choosing a representative sampling pool throughout the alphabet. Similarly, if a list is ordered by seniority (i.e., those with longest membership come first on the list), then by sampling across the entire listing a representative sampling pool will be generated that is uncorrelated with length of membership. As Henry (1990) notes, the surveyor should be careful to avoid choosing a sampling interval that coincides with any cyclical pattern inherent in the list. An added advantage of systematic sampling automatically occurs when de facto stratification results from lists that are ordered along some characteristic of interest, which in turn may lead to a reduction in sampling error (see Henry, 1990, p. 101).

Reverse directories can also be used to sample persons within small, localized geographic areas (e.g., neighborhoods) where RDD sampling would prove much too costly, providing that noncoverage error (due to missing households with unlisted numbers) would not invalidate the survey's purpose. To determine the number of households to sample per block, it is best to have a detailed street map available. If the map shows actual housing units, then proportional sampling can be done to represent the approximate population per block in the final sample. If this level of information is not readily available, a surveyor may simply count the number of block faces in the geographic sampling area and divide the desired size of the sampling pool by this amount. The quotient would then be used as the number of telephone numbers to sample per block. For example, suppose an evaluation researcher had a control neighborhood and a treatment neighborhood in which a sampling pool of 500 telephone numbers would be needed to complete 300 interviews in each neighborhood. If each neighborhood had approximately 100 block faces, then five telephone numbers should be drawn in a random or systematic fashion from each block (this approach assumes that the population and/or the number of households per block face is approximately equal). The proper use of a reverse directory also requires that accurate information is available about the starting and ending address number on each block; thus the advantage provided by a detailed street-level map. (These maps are often available from local government planning departments.)

At present many organizations have their employee or membership lists computerized. In such cases, their computer software may be capable of drawing a random or systematic sample from the entire listing or may be used to generate a data base for manipulation by other software packages. In addition, some reverse directory data bases are available in computer-readable form (e.g., on diskettes).

Commercial List Vendors

During the 1980s there was a growth in businesses that provide lists for purchase. Of special interest to telephone survey researchers, these lists include city telephone directories, master address lists, subscriber lists, and client lists. Companies also exist that create a variety of telephone survey sampling pools for paying clients, including pools for RDD surveying. Furthermore, many of these lists can be generated so that they are stratified along some characteristic of interest to the surveyor (e.g., zip codes).

As attractive as this may appear, a surveyor must be cautious in using lists prepared by an outside party, with special concern shown to possible coverage errors in the lists. If one chooses to purchase a list to serve as one's sampling pool or from which to generate a sampling pool, the careful surveyor also must be a careful consumer; that is, make certain that all questions are answered to your satisfaction regarding exactly how the master list and the purchased sampling pool are created. For example, from where does the firm get their data base information; how often is the list updated; and what coverage errors does the firm acknowledge to exist in its own list? Remember that random sampling from a "master list" may not represent a probability sample of the target population if coverage error is associated with the manner in which the master list was assembled. In sum, I agree with Lepkowski's (1988) advice that "it is often unacceptable for this critical phase of survey operations [i.e., generating one's sampling pool] to be out of [the surveyor's] direct control" (p. 79).

However, due to the convenience that commercial lists afford, a prudent middle ground for those who decide to use such lists would be to try to modify the purchased list to lessen the likelihood of contributing to total survey error through its unmodified use. For example, one could buy a list of assigned telephone numbers of the general population in a specific sampling area from a commercial vendor and then randomly replace the last two digits on each number or apply one of the added-digit(s) techniques. This may be far less expensive than gathering the prefix and suffix information from scratch and would help to offset the problem of non-coverage of unlisted telephone numbers inherent in the purchased list. In another example, a surveyor may choose to purchase a list of names and telephone numbers and then work to reduce noncontacts due to numbers that do not reach the sampled individual by having the research staff aggressively track new numbers. This would reduce the threat of nonresponse error which would otherwise result from using the purchased list without any systematic follow-up.

MIXED MODE SAMPLING POOLS

As noted in Chapter 1, the past decade has seen a growing interest in surveys that combine more than one mode of sampling and data collection. The appeal of combining different survey modes (personal, telephone, mail) follows the reasoning that total survey error may be reduced if the limitations of one mode are offset by the strengths of another (see Dillman,

Sangster, & Rockwood, 1992; Dillman & Tarnai, 1988). For the surveyor who is planning the manner in which a sampling pool will be generated, mixed mode may require additional time and resources to assemble the sampling frame(s). For example, a survey of a specific neighborhood that does not conform well with telephone prefix geographic boundaries might employ a dual-frame approach by combining the mail and telephone modes. The sampling pool for the part to be done by telephone could be generated from a reverse directory; this would cover only households with listed telephone numbers at the time the directory was printed. The sampling pool for the part to be done via mail could be generated from block/address maps from the city's housing department. Here, it would be necessary to eliminate possible duplicate households sampled via both methods. Furthermore, as each of the households in the telephone sampling pool has a listed address, advance letters could be mailed to inform residents they have been selected for the telephone survey. The mail part would require several follow-up mailings to reduce nonresponse and should include an item asking whether or not the household has a telephone and, if so, if the number is listed or unlisted. This information would allow the surveyor to investigate any differences that may exist in the data associated with each mode.

Telephone surveyors considering the mixed mode approach should follow the growing research literature on mixed mode surveys to learn under which circumstances the potential for gains is "justified when costs and other error considerations are taken into account" (Lepkowski, 1988, p. 98).

The reader should not confuse the issue of mixed mode sampling pools with a telephone survey that also uses an advance letter that is mailed to potential respondents before they are called by interviewers (discussed in Chapter 4). If, for example, a telephone survey sampling pool was generated from a list of all members of a professional organization and the list also contained the individuals' mailing addresses, a surveyor would be wise to alert the persons in the sampling pool that they have been chosen to participate in a forthcoming telephone survey. In this example, combining mail contact with telephone interviewing is advisable, but it does not constitute a mixed mode (or dual-frame) sampling pool.

SAMPLING POOL SIZE

In an ideal telephone survey every number dialed would be working, every selected respondent would be available for the interview at the time of the first call, and no respondent would refuse. Of course, nothing even remotely approaching this ideal ever happens with surveys. Every telephone sampling pool, even the most up-to-date list, will reach "wrong" numbers. Some small proportion of designated respondents are likely to never be available during the survey's field period. It is unlikely also that the refusal rate for most telephone surveys can be kept near zero (or even below 10%, for that matter).

The result of this attrition often requires a sampling pool that is far larger than the number of completed interviews desired. It is the surveyor's responsibility to choose a final sample size that is large enough to support the survey's purpose (i.e., one with low enough sampling error), but it is not the purpose of this text to fully advise the reader on how to make this decision. Other texts that deal with sampling error and statistical power should be consulted if the reader is unfamiliar with this decision-making process. For example, Sudman (1976) has an entire chapter, "How Big Should the Sample Be?", for those planning surveys designed to estimate some univariate population parameter. (As used by Sudman, the word *sample* refers to the number of completed interviews, not the size of the sampling pool that will be processed to achieve the completions.) For those whose survey is designed to measure bivariate and/or multivariate interrelationships, the notion of statistical power and sample size is addressed by Hays (1973) and Lipsey (1989).

For review, the reader is reminded that when a survey is designed to estimate the level at which some variable exists within a given population, probability sampling is employed, and all other potential sources of nonsampling error are constant, the degree of precision of the survey's measures will be enhanced as the sample size increases. In the case of a binomial variable (e.g., a survey item on abortion legislation that has a *favor* or *oppose* response) with a 50/50 split and with simple random sampling, a sample size of 100 will have a margin of error of approximately plus/minus 10 percentage points, at the 95% confidence interval. For a sample of 1,000 the sampling error decreases to approximately plus/minus 3 percentage points. With sample sizes approaching 10,000 it reduces to about plus/minus 1 percentage point. All these figures presume that sampling is done from an arbitrarily large population. If the size of the population being sampled is relatively small (i.e., 10,000 or less) the sampling error for a particular sample size begins to decrease as the size of the population itself decreases.

As mentioned before, those with a full CATI system (i.e., ones with appropriate software) may be able to avoid the need to generate the entire sampling pool before starting the survey. However, those using PAPI and many with CATI will want to generate a sufficiently large sampling pool for the entire survey before interviewing begins, but to release numbers from the pool on a daily basis and in a tightly controlled fashion (as discussed in Chapters 3 and 6).

If this approach is followed, one must be able to estimate an adequately sized sampling pool. The practical objective is to produce enough numbers in advance so that one does not have to do this a second, third, fourth time, or more. On the other hand, it is not cost-effective to generate an unnecessarily immense sampling pool, even when using a computer. To produce a realistic estimate of how many numbers are likely to be needed in a particular survey, one must answer the following questions:

1. What final sample size is desired?
2. What will be the likely hit-rate in the sampling pool for working numbers?
3. What proportion of working numbers will be screened out due to a priori respondent exclusion criteria?
4. What proportion of eligible respondents will be lost to the final sample due to nonresponse?

This information can then be used in the following formula to estimate the size of the sampling pool:

$$\text{ESTIMATED SIZE OF SAMPLING POOL} = (\text{FSS})/((\text{HR})(1\text{-REC})(1\text{-LE}))$$

Final Sample Size

The final sample size (FSS) is the number of completed interviews the surveyor has determined is needed for the purposes of the survey. As mentioned earlier, this is an important decision, based in part on the availability of resources to support data collection.

Hit-Rate

The hit-rate (HR) is an estimate of the proportion of telephone numbers in the sampling pool that is likely to be working and that will ring at appropriate locations (e.g., residences, not businesses). The hit-rate will vary across sampling areas. In the absence of knowledge gained from previous experience surveying a specific population, an adequate way to estimate HR is to gather comprehensive information from local telephone companies or local directories. For example, with a reverse directory, one can estimate the density of working numbers for each prefix in the sampling area. Here some knowledge of the proportion of numbers that is likely to be unlisted is also useful.

The experience of others can also provide safe estimates for the HR value. Groves and Kahn (1979) found in their national one-stage RDD sampling that approximately 20% of the numbers in their sampling pool reached residences. A large national RDD study NUSL completed in 1992 found 23% of Stage 1 numbers to be residential. In this latter case the value of HR would be .23. In my own experience with localized samples throughout various parts of the country, the HR value often ranges from .30-.50. For example, in the metropolitan Chicago area (the 312 and 708 area codes) most prefixes are very densely packed with residential numbers; thus, it is not unusual for a prefix to have been assigned to 4,000-6,000 residences out of a possible 10,000. In this case, HR would be in the .40-.60 range. As one moves farther from a central city, though, the HR value is likely to decrease, so it is best to gather information to make an estimate with each new sampling area.

Something else to keep in mind when estimating the HR value is the proportion of numbers likely to be nonresidential. In the 1992 RDD survey mentioned in the previous paragraph, NUSL found about a 2:1 ratio of residential to nonresidential telephone access lines in the United States.

Respondent Exclusion Criteria

Any respondent exclusion criteria (REC) that make certain persons or households ineligible will necessitate an increase in the size of the sampling pool. (It is important to understand that this does not contribute to a survey's nonresponse error, because these are persons or households that are not part of the surveyor's target population.) The REC value, which represents the proportion of households that will be excluded due to a priori selection criteria, is fairly easy to calculate but often requires recent census information for the sampling area. If, for example, only males over the age of 17 years can be interviewed, then approximately one third of all households will be excluded because persons fitting this demographic requirement will not live there. In this case the REC value would be .33. In many metropolitan areas a survey that must screen for senior citizens (adults over the age of 59 years) would find that about four out of every five residences reached via RDD would not have such a person living there. In this case the REC value would be .80.

RDD surveys designed to sample respondents within the boundaries of particular communities often have to employ geographic screeners. In these cases the surveyor must be able to estimate the REC value for those who will be reached by RDD but excluded because they live outside the sampling area.

Many surveys will not be targeted to some specialized segment of the general population, other than those persons over the age of 17 years (i.e., all adults). As such, the effective REC for many surveys is at or near zero (.00). But as eligibility criteria become more restrictive, this value can grow and may eventually rule against the use of a sampling design that uses telephone numbers from the general population. For many varied practical reasons, I use .10-.20 as the REC range below which I begin to caution those contemplating telephone surveys to possibly consider other approaches to sampling. Of course this is highly dependent on the purpose of the survey and the available resources. For example, NUSL recently planned an RDD survey that would have an REC value of .98; that is, an estimated 49 in 50 households would be *excluded* because of a lack of an eligible respondent.

Loss of Eligibles

The loss of eligibles (LE) due to nonresponse is the final factor one must consider when estimating the size of the sampling pool. Even with the best group of well-supervised and experienced telephone interviewers, the LE value is likely to range from .15-.25 with the general public due largely to refusals. Experience shows that as sampling is concentrated more and more in central cities, and especially if the quality of interviewing is not top-notch, LE can reach or even exceed .50. In this case, one must question the validity of conducting the survey in the first place given the likely size of the nonresponse error (see Groves, 1989).

In contrast, when interviewing special populations the LE value may be very low. For example, for a 1992 national survey of criminal justice practitioners conducted at NUSL, an LE value of .05 was planned, but a value of zero (.00) was achieved; that is, *everyone* in the sampling pool was interviewed! (The issue of how to try to minimize survey nonresponse, and thus the LE value, is discussed in Chapters 5 and 6.)

Estimating Sampling Pool Size

In a survey that was planned as this original edition of the book was written, a client of NUSL wanted 300 interviews completed in Chicago via RDD with white or black males of non-Jewish and non-Arab descent, who were 25 years of age or older. For that survey, FSS equaled 300. The HR value for Chicago was approximately .50. Based on the respondent screening that would be needed once a residence was contacted, REC was approximately .50. Finally, with this exclusively male sample in the city of Chicago, the effective LE was estimated at .40. Using the formula,

ESTIMATED SIZE OF SAMPLING POOL = $(300)/((.50)(1-.50)(1-.4)) = 2,000$

for this survey it was estimated that approximately 2,000 telephone numbers would be needed for processing by interviewers in the course of completing the 300 interviews. As a contingency, however, my own preference is to further inflate an estimate by 10%; thus, in this example a sampling pool of 2,200 numbers was advised.

EXERCISES

Exercise 2.1: Generate a sampling pool (manually) of 20 telephone numbers using a random numbers table. Use the following set of prefixes in equal proportions: 328-, 475-, 491-, and 866-.

Exercise 2.2: Generate a sampling pool (manually) of 100 telephone numbers using a random numbers table. Use the following prefixes and leading suffix digits; also, stratify the sampling pool by prefix using the proportions shown in parentheses: 328-1 (10%), 328-3 (20%), 475-6 (6%), 475-7 (5%), 475-8 (4%), 475-9 (10%), 491-2 (22%), 866-0 (15%), and 866-1 (8%). (Or write a computer program in BASIC or another language to generate this sampling pool.)

Exercise 2.3: Estimate the prevalence of unpublished telephone numbers in a local municipality. Use the local telephone directory for that municipality and the most recent census data on the number of households in the municipality.

Exercise 2.4: Calculate the estimated size of a sampling pool that should be generated for the following survey, using the local municipality in Exercise 2.3: In the survey 500 interviews will be completed with one adult, 18-29 years of age, per household. Assume that 1 in every 5 eligible respondents will refuse to participate and that 1 in every 10 of the other eligible respondents will never be reached to complete the interview during the time the survey is being conducted.

3

Processing Telephone Survey Sampling Pools

Chapter 2 explained how sampling pools for telephone surveys are produced; this chapter discusses the controlled use of the telephone numbers in the sampling pool. The primary goal in controlling the processing of telephone survey sampling pools is to finish data collection with as representative a sample of the sampling frame as possible by reducing the potential threat of nonresponse error. It should be noted that noncoverage error should not be affected by the manner in which a sampling pool is processed, but rather by the manner in which the sampling frame was chosen to represent the target population and/or the manner in which the sampling pool was generated from the sampling frame.

This book takes the position that the major advantage of telephone surveys compared with other survey modes is the centralized control that the telephone affords over the entire data collection endeavor. The care with which the sampling pool is processed by interviewers and supervisory personnel is a critical facet of this control of quality.

Chapter 3 begins with an overview of why and how sampling pools are controlled. The use of a call-sheet, or its on-screen equivalent in CATI, is then explained. A call-sheet is a form that is assigned to each telephone number released from the sampling pool. Included in this section is a detailed discussion of various outcomes (dispositions) that may occur when interviewers dial telephone numbers, and an explanation of how interviewers should handle different dispositions. It is these dispositions that are used by supervisory personnel (or programmed into CATI) to determine whether (and when) to have interviewers redial a telephone number. Next is a section on a relatively new and evolving approach to controlling the processing of call-sheets that result in refusals through the use of a *refusal report form*. The following section provides a perspective on the pattern of dispositions that may be expected when processing sampling pools and a discussion of how the processing of sampling pools relates to various response rates associated with telephone surveys. The chapter ends with a perspective on processing sampling pools in mixed mode surveys and a summary of the potential advantages for reducing nonresponse error afforded by CATI systems.

ISSUES IN CONTROLLING THE SAMPLING POOL

The primary reason for having a formal system to control the use of numbers released from the sampling pool is to avoid the considerable nonresponse that would likely result if interviewers were allowed simply to choose telephone numbers from the sampling pool at whim. For example, only through use of a highly routinized system will harder-to-contact respondents get called back an appropriate number of times. If this is not done, the final sample will be disproportionately composed of easier-to-contact respondents. Because harder-to-contact respondents in a survey of the general population are more likely to be younger and male, and easier-to-contact respondents are more likely to be older and female, the potential threat of nonresponse error attributable to noncontacts would be increased and the external validity (generalizability) of the final sample may be compromised. This follows from the fact that demographic factors associated with noncontacts (e.g., age and gender) are often correlated with the topical focus of a survey. A similar concern exists with potential nonresponse error associated with refusals. To try to lessen these problems a surveyor must employ a formal system of control over the numbers that are dialed by interviewers.

Such a system also improves interviewer efficiency by removing the burden of scheduling callbacks from interviewers. This permits interviewers to concentrate on doing their best possible interviewing, as opposed to also being concerned with determining which numbers should be processed. Furthermore, if efforts are made to convert initial refusals (i.e., calling back to persuade those who initially refused to complete the interview), these call-sheets can be individually rescheduled at times deemed best by the supervisory personnel controlling the sampling pool. In sum, by having supervisory personnel retain total responsibility for providing interviewers with numbers from the sampling pool, any bias that could result if interviewers chose numbers for themselves is more likely to be avoided.

When a PAPI telephone survey is conducted the control and sorting of processed telephone numbers from the sampling pool is done manually. This approach is addressed in detail in this chapter. With the manual approach, there are three basic steps to controlling a sampling pool:

1. Interviewers should be given a relatively small group of telephone numbers with which to start the interviewing session.

2. A supervisor will need to provide additional numbers to interviewers during the interviewing session.

3. Before the next session begins the group of numbers that were processed during the previous session must be sorted. Experience strongly recommends that one person be given responsibility for this final step.

The preferred way for this level of control to be instituted is through the use of a separate call-sheet (as shown in Figure 3.1) for each telephone number released from the sampling pool. By having a unique call-sheet for each number dialed by interviewers, a history (or call record) can be constructed that explains what happened each time a particular number was dialed. Even with CATI there is an on-screen equivalent of the call-sheet that controls and facilitates interviewers' processing of the numbers in the sampling pool. As noted later in this chapter, where CATI differs from PAPI in this aspect of the survey process is the automatic decision rules that can be programmed into the system that replace some of the human decision making needed with PAPI.

The reader should note that the approaches to controlling the sampling pool described in this chapter are in part a matter of personal choice. I have successfully employed these paper-and-pencil, hand-sorted systems for nearly 15 years. Other survey organizations that do PAPI telephone surveys use similar systems, but not always with such a detailed set of disposition codes nor with as much demanding follow-through (i.e., reprocessing) of individual telephone numbers.

The approaches presented here are not the only valid systems that can be employed. After reading this chapter one could choose to devise a modified system to best meet her or his own needs. The important point remains: Even with CATI, quality telephone surveys necessitate a *constant and attentive human oversight* of the processing of telephone numbers released from the sampling pool, although without CATI the time demands on supervisory personnel are greater.

USING THE CALL-SHEET
TO CONTROL THE SAMPLING POOL

Every telephone number released from the sampling pool should be printed on a separate piece of paper, the call-sheet, on which interviewers

User Supplied Title

Telephone Number ###-####			Questionnaire #: __ __ __ __	
Contact attempts	Date	Time	Disposition code	Interviewer ID
1	__/__	__:__	__ __	__ __
2	__/__	__:__	__ __	__ __
3	__/__	__:__	__ __	__ __
4	__/__	__:__	__ __	__ __
5	__/__	__:__	__ __	__ __
6	__/__	__:__	__ __	__ __
7	__/__	__:__	__ __	__ __
8	__/__	__:__	__ __	__ __
9	__/__	__:__	__ __	__ __
10	__/__	__:__	__ __	__ __

NOTES

1. _____
2. _____
3. _____
4. _____
5. _____
6. _____
7. _____
8. _____
9. _____
10. _____

Figure 3.1. Example of a Call-Sheet.

record information that allows supervisory personnel to decide what to do with each number that has been processed. Some organizations refer to this sheet as the *call record*, others designate it the *interviewer report form* (IRF).

To be certain of the meaning of the phrase, "released from the sampling pool," the reader is reminded that it is not necessary to process all numbers in the sampling pool. As discussed in Chapter 2, it is recommended that a sampling pool be generated in its entirety in advance of interviewing, except in those cases in which a CATI system can do this simultaneously with interviewing (although not all CATI software has this capability). Telephone numbers from the sampling pool are then released to interviewers only as needed. To reduce the possibility of nonresponse error and thereby maximize the external validity of the final sample, all numbers that are released from the sampling pool should be fully processed (i.e., called back an adequate number of times). Neither nonresponse error nor total survey error is inflated when one does not release all the numbers originally generated to reach the desired number of completions, assuming the numbers that were released are a random subset of all those generated.

Figure 3.1 is an example of the basic call-sheet used at NUSL. It is modeled after the form used by the Survey Research Laboratory at the University of Illinois and is similar to that used by many other survey organizations. Its purpose is to provide interviewers with a formalized structure to record important information about every dialing of each telephone number that is released from the sampling pool.

The information to be written on the call-sheet shown in Figure 3.1 includes the date, time, and the disposition of each dialing. The *disposition* refers to the coded outcome of each dialing (e.g., ring-no-answer, busy, out-of-order, refusal, completed, callback, etc.). The interviewer is also expected to record her or his ID number with each dialing. Finally, the form provides space for annotation that can be extremely helpful both to the person who sorts the call-sheets and to any interviewer who may subsequently redial the telephone number.

As will be discussed in Chapter 4, these call-sheets may be paired with another sheet that contains the introductory spiel for the survey and a respondent selection procedure. Call-sheets are attached to a questionnaire only after an interview has been completed. As shown in Figure 3.1, the telephone number can be printed in the upper left corner and space is provided toward the upper right so that a unique questionnaire ID number (or case number) can be assigned later. Call-sheets for different surveys should be printed with different titles, and on differently colored paper when a group of interviewers is conducting two or more surveys simultaneously.

Prior to the actual dialing of a telephone number, an interviewer should record the date and time in the appropriate columns across the next open row of call-attempts. The date need only be the month and day. Ideally, a wall clock should be positioned in a centralized location easily seen by all interviewers. Finally, before placing the call, the interviewer should also record her or his ID; in most cases this will be a two-digit number, but with small groups of interviewers, initials are acceptable. (With CATI, all this information can be automatically recorded for each dialing.)

It is important that interviewers record the date and time of the call because this information can aid in subsequent decisions that are made about the call-sheet. For example, because call-attempts are spaced throughout the period that the survey is being fielded (conducted), having the date and time recorded allows supervisory personnel to determine best when to reprocess a number. In some cases, especially with numbers that consistently ring without answer, the person controlling the sampling pool must hold aside a call-sheet for a particular day and time.

Accountability is the primary reason for having interviewers record their ID number. This allows supervisory personnel to determine which interviewer placed a particular call. Knowing such information is critical to the successful resolution of problems that inevitably arise. With PAPI, it also provides the means whereby an interviewer's productivity can be estimated. (CATI provides considerable potential for producing statistics on interviewer productivity.) Apart from this, the psychology underlying such a system reinforces the notion that high-quality work is expected from individual interviewers and that their performance is constantly monitored.

The most crucial information that is recorded on the call-sheet is the disposition code, indicating the outcome of each dialing. It is through inspection of the disposition code that call-sheets can be quickly and efficiently sorted after each interviewing session. The set of disposition categories and their associated numerical codes that are described in the following pages are fairly exhaustive, and can easily be collapsed into broader categories if a surveyor so chooses. An important point for most telephone surveys is that some numerical coding scheme should be used by interviewers in order to enhance the ability of supervisory personnel to control the sampling pool. Use of such a formal system also serves to reinforce the professionalism that should be expected of interviewers.

Table 3.1 presents one such coding scheme. The reader should note that the numerical codes that are assigned to different dispositions in this table are arbitrary; that is, there is nothing special about this particular numbering.

The set of dispositions listed in Table 3.1 is fairly typical for surveys of the general population that employ a formal respondent selection procedure within each household that is contacted. A set of codes like this should be used regardless of whether the sampling pool was generated from a list or RDD. Depending on the particular purpose of the survey, the surveyor may need to employ additional disposition codes. For example, when a panel survey is conducted (i.e., one in which the same respondents are reinterviewed after some passage of time, such as one year later), disposition codes are needed for the different reasons that a person might no longer be reached via the telephone number he or she had been reached during the previous wave of the panel.

For the following explanation of the dispositions shown in Table 3.1 and elsewhere, I will refer to the supervisory personnel responsible for controlling the overall processing of telephone numbers as the sampling pool *controller*. As mentioned earlier, I recommend that one person be charged with this responsibility, which includes determining when to

Table 3.1

Example of Disposition Codes for Controlling a Sampling Pool

Disposition code	Explanation
10	No answer after seven rings
11	Busy, after one immediate redial
12	Answering machine (residence)
13	Household language barrier
14	Answered by nonresident
15	Household refusal; use 15H for immediate hang-up without comment
20	Disconnected or other nonworking
21	Temporarily disconnected
22	Business, other nonresidence
23	No one meets eligibility criteria
30	Contact only; use 30A for appointment
31	Selected respondent temporarily unavailable
32	Selected respondent unavailable during field period
33	Selected respondent unavailable due to physical/mental disability
34	Language barrier with selected respondent
35	Refusal by selected respondent
36	Partial interview; use 36R for refusal
37	Completed interview

release particular call-sheets to interviewers, when to reschedule the processing of a call-sheet, and when to remove a call-sheet from further processing. This latter decision will depend in part on how many callbacks have been budgeted for interviewers to make with ring-no-answers, initial refusals, and hard-to-contact respondents.

Ring-No-Answer

In the majority of times that interviewers dial telephone numbers, especially with RDD sampling, they will not complete an interview. In many of these dialings they will not reach anyone at all—the telephone will ring without being answered. Several RDD surveys conducted in the past 10 years by NUSL show that between one third and one half of all dialings made by interviewers result in the number ringing but not being answered.

As shown in Table 3.1, a disposition code representing the ring-no-answer outcome is assigned by interviewers after a predetermined number of rings have elapsed without the telephone being answered. The number of rings interviewers should allow before hanging up depends on the surveyor's preference. On the low side, four or five rings should occur before an interviewer hangs up (see Frey, 1989, p. 228; Smead & Wilcox, 1980), although it is not cost-effective for interviews to allow numbers to ring many more times. At NUSL interviewers are expected to allow a telephone to ring seven times before coding it a ring-no-answer. An exception would be telephone numbers that have been dialed on several previous occasions without ever being answered. In this case it is wise to have interviewers allow the telephone to ring in excess of 10 times before hanging up.

Ring-no-answers may be reprocessed once per session, session after session, until a predetermined number of callbacks has been made. The number of callbacks that should be made is based in part on the resources available to support the survey and on the length of the field period. In general, the fewer callbacks that are budgeted the greater the proportion of numbers that will ring yet never be answered. The difficult trade-off a surveyor faces is to spend relatively more resources on additional callbacks which yield diminishing returns the more callbacks that are made (i.e., proportionately fewer households will be reached on the 15th call than on the 10th, fewer on the 20th than on the 15th, and so on). Groves and Kahn (1979) estimated that only 5% of the numbers dialed more than 12 times in their large national methodological test of RDD sampling were households. This low hit-rate of households among numbers unanswered after many dialings is routinely encountered in many large-scale government-sponsored RDD studies (Maklan & Waksberg, 1988). Yet potential nonresponse error associated with these hardest-to-contact households could contribute substantially to total survey error if they are not interviewed. An option that is not always viable or cost-effective is to systematically contact telephone companies to determine the status of numbers that are never answered. The interested reader is referred to Sebold's (1988) more detailed discussion of the perplexing issue of how to handle unanswered numbers in telephone surveys.

Busy Signals

In most cases, a busy signal is a positive outcome because it usually means that someone can eventually be reached via the number. Busy signals should be coded as busy after the interviewer has immediately and carefully redialed the number. The reason to have interviewers do this is to make certain they dialed correctly the first time and also to take advantage of the slight chance that whoever was using the telephone was in the process of finishing the conversation.

At the surveyor's discretion, interviewers can be permitted to redial busy numbers later in an interviewing session (e.g., after 30 minutes or so). If this practice is followed, there must be a limit on how often the interviewer can call back, otherwise the disposition code column of the call-sheet will get filled quickly with "busys." I believe it is reasonable to have interviewers redial busy numbers once or twice in a session.

A potential problem that must be avoided is misidentifying a "fast-busy" signal. This is a tone used by some telephone companies to indicate a nonworking number or busy circuits due to heavy call volume. If interviewers are alerted to these signals, they are less likely to confuse them with normal busy signals and thereby will conserve time that would otherwise be wasted on unnecessary redialings. A fast-busy will normally be coded as a nonworking number and the controller will remove the call-sheet from further processing. An exception would be surveys conducted in areas where telephone circuits are often overloaded. In this case, it behooves the surveyor to use a separate code for fast-busys so they can be called back during another session to confirm their status.

Answering Machines

As the cost of telephone answering machines has dropped dramatically, more of the public have come to use them. In 1992, market research estimates suggested that half of U.S. households have them, with the proportion increasing annually. My own research on households with answering machines finds those most likely to own them (and use them) are adults under the age of 30 years, whites, and those with higher incomes and education. The vast majority (70%-75%) of those with an answering machine report they have the device so as not to miss incoming calls (a group some refer to as "connectors") as opposed to having the machine primarily to screen out unwanted calls ("cocooners"). Furthermore, answering machine ownership appears basically unrelated to completion rates and to the number of callbacks it takes to achieve a completion in surveys that routinely employ 10 or more callbacks.

If the message on an answering machine indicates that a business has been reached and the survey is one of residences, then the disposition code for nonresidence should be used, rather than the disposition code for an answering machine (see Table 3.1). For times when the interviewer is uncertain who has been reached, or suspects or knows it is a residence, answering machines deserve their own unique disposition codes since this informs the controller that an interview may eventually be completed at this telephone number.

A decision with answering machines is whether or not to have interviewers leave a message. To date, there is no definitive research to advise on this issue. My recommendation is to have interviewers do so in order to personalize the contact—but the message should be brief, polite, and standardized. In other words, all interviewers should be instructed what to say when they reach a residential answering machine. The message should be similar to the introduction that is used in the survey: It should identify the survey group and the purpose and importance of the survey, and should alert the resident that a callback will be made.

The controller must give special attention to those numbers that reach answering machines. By looking at time-of-day and/or day-of-week patterns of call-attempts and dispositions on the call-sheet, a telephone number that has consistently reached an answering machine can be held aside for recycling on certain days or at certain times that have not been tried before. This will depend partly on the length of the survey's field period.

Household Language Barrier

In general, the closer a survey's sampling area is to a central city, the more often interviewers will reach households whose telephones are answered by persons who do not speak English, or at least cannot speak it well enough to complete an English-language interview accurately.

There is some reason to believe that on certain occasions "no-English" is used as a ploy to avoid speaking to the interviewer. If this occurs it actually constitutes a refusal if the person can speak English better than he or she admits. Unfortunately, there is no standardized way for an interviewer to determine if this has happened.

When language appears to be a barrier, interviewers should code it as such, without arguing with the person with whom they are speaking, even if they suspect the person's veracity. If resources allow, the controller should recycle these numbers during another interviewing session on the chance that the second dialing will reach a person who can (and will) communicate in English. This can be especially useful in surveys that utilize a systematic within-household selection procedure (as discussed in Chapter 4), as the person ultimately selected as the respondent may be English-speaking.

For surveys that employ Spanish-language in addition to English-language interviewers, NUSL's experience with Chicago's fairly large and somewhat undocumented Hispanic population has shown that more than half of all interviews conducted with persons who identify themselves as Hispanic can be done accurately in English. Thus, the problem of missing non-English-speaking households in the general population is often a relatively small one, even when a survey cannot afford non-English interviewing. (Non-English interviewing requires that the questionnaire be translated and printed in a second language. Interviewers who are bilingual must not translate questions on their own from an English version. If this were done, all standardization of question form would be lost because non-English-speaking respondents would no longer hear the same wording across all bilingual interviewers.)

Answered by Nonresident

On rare occasions a telephone is answered by someone who does not live at the household and the interviewer is told that none of the occupants are at home. This happens with baby-sitters, house sitters, cleaning persons, and friends or relatives who have checked in while the residents are away on vacation. In such instances interviewers should explain the reason they are calling and try to determine when a resident will return. This information should be written in the notes section of the call-sheet. The controller can then have an interviewer reprocess the number on the appropriate day, assuming the field period extends that long.

Household Refusals

In telephone surveys of the general public, the majority of refusals occur shortly after the telephone has been answered and before a designated respondent has been selected from within the household (see Collins, Sykes, Wilson, & Blackshaw, 1988). Thus, they are coded as household refusals. Research suggests that this category typically includes between two thirds and three fourths of initial refusals (Lavrakas, Merkle, & Bauman, 1992). In all cases interviewers should write an explanation of the nature of the refusal on the call-sheet. (As explained later in this chapter, a surveyor may choose to employ a refusal report form which interviewers would complete each time they experienced a refusal.)

People often say, "we're not interested," "we don't have time," or "we don't do surveys," and sometimes merely hang up without any response. These reasons, respectively, account for approximately 40%, 20%, 10%, and 10% of refusals (Lavrakas et al., 1992). In the case of outright hang-ups, some proportion of no-comment hang-ups may be at non-English households. Therefore, interviewers should be instructed to code such outcomes with a separate disposition code (e.g., the 15H code shown in Table 3.1).

This allows the controller the option of recycling these call-sheets with bilingual interviewers, if such interviewers are available.

From the standpoint of processing the sample, the surveyor should make an a priori decision about attempts to convert refusals. From experience, it appears that regardless of what people give as their reason for refusing it most often was the timing of the call that was problematic. An interviewer may have reached the household at an inconvenient time and/or the person answering the telephone may simply have been in an uncooperative mood.

As discussed in Chapter 5, interviewers must be trained to be "politely persistent" when someone refuses before giving up on that particular call attempt. Once an interviewer senses that a particular dialing will result in a refusal, however, he or she should terminate the exchange by commenting along the following lines: "OK, I'm sorry we bothered you at this time."

For surveys with lengthy field periods (two or more weeks), many survey organizations have a standard practice of processing household refusals a second time after a delay of about a week, on the chance that the telephone will be answered by someone willing to cooperate. Strong (but not adamant) refusals probably should be routed to interviewers with a special knack of eliciting cooperation. At NUSL the practice is that any household in which an interviewer is explicitly told, ". . . and don't call back!" should not be included in refusal conversion attempts. As discussed later, the use of a refusal report form (RRF) can be especially helpful to interviewers who make callbacks to these numbers. Whatever decision is followed, household refusals merit special attention as the sampling pool is being processed because the refusal rate contributes to potential nonresponse error and thereby can threaten the external validity of the survey.

Nonworking Numbers

The practices of telephone companies operating within the sampling area determine the ease with which nonworking numbers are identified. Closer to central cities, most telephone companies use a variety of recorded messages that inform the caller, "the number you have dialed is disconnected," or something to that effect. In other instances no connection will be made or an unusual noise will be heard. When sampling in some rural areas nonworking numbers may simply ring without answer.

After the disposition code for ring-no-answer, the nonworking disposition code is typically the second most frequently used code in RDD surveys of the general public. Whenever an interviewer dials a number that is not in operation the nonworking disposition code should be recorded on the respective call-sheet. This includes those dialings in which a recorded message informs the interviewer that the dialed number has been changed (and a new number is given) or that calls are being taken by some other telephone number. For most RDD surveys, interviewers should *not* dial changed numbers, because it may distort sampling probabilities in unknown ways.

In most instances, once a nonworking disposition occurs the controller removes the call-sheet from further processing. In an RDD survey with a comfortably sized sampling pool, there is little reason to redial a nonworking number despite the chance that it was misdialed the first time or that it subsequently has been assigned to a household. This is because dialing mistakes and the chance of reassignment should be very rare and basically random processes that should not add coverage bias to the final sample. Furthermore, redialing all nonworking numbers is not cost-effective.

Temporarily Disconnected

Recorded messages that inform interviewers that a telephone number is temporarily out of service or is "being checked for trouble" should have a separate disposition code from nonworking. The controller should recycle the call-sheet a second time after a few days, providing the field period of the survey is long enough to justify this effort.

Nonresidential

For surveys of the general public, interviews must not be conducted at businesses or other nonresidential locations (e.g., hospitals, libraries, government offices, etc.). Depending on the sampling area, it is likely that between one fourth and one third of all working telephone numbers will be nonresidential; thus, this disposition is fairly common in RDD sampling pools.

Interviewers should know how to explain why an interview of the general public cannot be conducted at nonresidential numbers: It violates probability sampling assumptions underlying surveys of the citizenry. Whenever an answering machine indicates that a business or other nonresidence has been reached, the call-sheet should be coded as nonresidential. If the high-pitched screech or hiss of a modem or fax machine is heard, a nonresidential code might well be listed on the call-sheet, although in some instances these may be residences that also use their line for business purposes.

Differentiating residences from nonresidences is complicated by call-forwarding technology, whereby one telephone number can be programmed to ring at another. In 1992 approximately 1 in 20 households nationwide subscribed to this service. In an RDD survey, for example, a residential number might be dialed that is forwarded to a business or vice versa. In each of these instances, it is the status of the number dialed that determines the disposition, not the location at which it is answered. If a business number is forwarded to a residence it should be coded as nonresidential and no interview should be conducted. If a residential number is forwarded to a business, an interview preferably should be conducted *at the residence* at some later time. As discussed in Chapter 4, alert interviewers are likely to detect these anomalies as part of the standard process whereby they verify the number they have dialed. Call-sheets with a nonresidential disposition are removed from further processing.

No Eligibles

Depending upon the particular respondent selection requirements of a telephone survey (see Chapter 4), in some instances households will be reached that contain no eligible respondent. This outcome should be recorded on the call-sheet and the controller should remove it from further processing.

When conducting a general population survey with adults over 17 years of age, interviewers will occasionally reach households that purportedly have no one that old living there. Because in most of these instances interviewers will be speaking with a child, these call-sheets, also coded "no eligibles," should be recycled by the controller a second time during a later interviewing session. After a second "no eligibles" contact at a household the controller may decide to remove the call-sheet from further processing.

Contact Only

For most surveys, less than half of all completed interviews occur on the first dialing and this proportion appears to be continuing to decrease, albeit slowly, each passing year. Whenever an interviewer reaches a household, uses the standard introductory spiel and respondent selection procedure, and is told that the designated respondent is not available at that time, the call-sheet should be coded with the "contact-only" disposition; that is, this outcome is not treated as a refusal. On these occasions it is critical that interviewers try to determine the best time to reach the respondent and record this information on the call-sheet; for example, "after 9:00 p.m." or "on weekends only." In this way the controller can make an informed judgment about when to recycle the call-sheet. Furthermore, interviewers should note on the call-sheet the gender, name, or any other identifying information about the designated respondent to facilitate the work of the interviewer who calls subsequently.

Occasionally an interviewer will be able to schedule a callback at a specific time. When this happens it is often helpful to have a unique disposition code (e.g., 30A in Table 3.1) to assist the controller in identifying these call-sheets and to assure that they are reprocessed at the correct time.

Temporarily Unavailable

A separate disposition code should be used to differentiate respondents who will be unavailable for several days or longer from those who are not home at the particular time of an interviewer's call (as discussed above). This may be due to brief illnesses, short vacations, or business trips. Providing the field period of the survey extends past the date these respondents will be available, the controller can hold aside those call-sheets until the appropriate date for reprocessing.

Permanently Unavailable

In contrast to a temporary state, there are instances when respondents are unavailable until after the end of the survey's field period (e.g., an extended vacation or work-related travel out of the country). In these cases interviewers can code the disposition as permanently unavailable and the controller can remove these call-sheets from further processing, unless the field period is later extended longer than originally planned.

Disability Barrier

Occasionally a person who meets demographic selection criteria (e.g., age and gender) is chosen as the respondent but due to some physical or mental disability is not capable of participating in the survey. This disposition includes a respondent who will be hospitalized beyond the survey field period. When such an outcome is encountered the controller can often stop processing the call-sheet, although the surveyor should make an a priori decision about whether or not to pursue another respondent within the household, if one exists. This latter decision should be consistent with the survey's overall sampling design (see Henry, 1990).

Sometimes, however, the incapacity is of a temporary nature (e.g., the respondent is intoxicated). In this case the interviewer should not conduct an interview but should note on the call-sheet that the disability barrier is only temporary. The controller should then recycle the call-sheet at some later date.

Respondent Language Barrier

As previously described, a separate disposition code is assigned to those call-sheets in which language makes it impossible to determine if there is an eligible respondent who speaks English. In other instances an interviewer will succeed in identifying a designated respondent within a household only to learn that *that* person cannot speak English. For example, an English-speaking young adult (who lives with her or his parents) may answer the telephone and complete the respondent selection sequence with the interviewer. The sequence in that household may choose the young adult's father, who in turn may not be able to speak English well enough to participate in the interview. This outcome might be coded as a respondent language barrier with the controller removing this call-sheet from further processing.

As with the disability barrier outcome, the surveyor should make an a priori decision, consistent with the sampling design, that determines whether or not another English-speaking resident in the household should be selected. For example, if the survey's target population is all English-speaking residents within an sampling area, then only English-speaking residents should be considered when the interviewer administers the respondent selection criteria (see Chapter 4). Coverage error is not increased when a non-English-speaking adult is first selected (actually by mistake) and then not interviewed because, in this example, the target population is limited to English-speaking adults. However, coverage error may be increased if another person who spoke English and was a household member was not afforded a chance of being sampled.

Refusal by Selected Respondent

In surveys that use a procedure to select a specific respondent from within a household, a refusal to participate will sometimes occur with the designated respondent; this accounts for about a third of initial refusals in RDD surveys. When this happens, a respondent refusal code should be recorded on the call-sheet. This outcome differs from the case in which the refusal occurs at the household level prior to the selection of the designated respondent.

It is important for the controller to be able to differentiate household refusals from respondent refusals, as the latter may be harder to convert since the refusal was given by the person who should be interviewed, and not by a gatekeeper within the household. As with all refusals, interviewers should be encouraged to write a brief explanation about the nature of the refusal or to complete an RRF if such a form is used (as discussed later). This information can be very helpful to the controller in judging how best (if at all) to reprocess the call-sheet and to other interviewers in judging how to be more persuasive if subsequent attempts are made to try to convert a particular refusal.

Partial Interview

Once an interview begins, it is very likely that a good interviewer can persuade a reluctant respondent to complete it. There are, however, instances in which the respondent cannot or will not continue through to the end of the questionnaire.

In the first case, something may occur during the interview that makes it infeasible for the respondent to finish at that time; for example, the respondent's baby will not stop crying. If handled properly by the interviewer, these respondents are usually quite willing to be called back at another time to complete the interview. This circumstance should be coded as a partial interview and the interviewer should note on the call-sheet when to call back. The controller should then make certain that the recontact is made at the appropriate time and, if at all possible, by the original interviewer.

The second type, in which the respondent refuses to go on and refuses to reschedule a time for a callback, should be also be coded as a partial interview and the interviewer should note that this is really a refusal by using a separate designation (such as the 36R in Table 3.1). In this case, an RRF should be completed if such a form is used. Experience indicates that these types of partials are often elderly respondents who get tired and/or become unsettled during the course of the interview. Fortunately, these types of partials do not occur often with good interviewers. When they do occur the controller may want to discuss with the original interviewer the wisdom of a callback after reviewing the call-sheet (and RRF if one is available).

It is possible that a particular partial may have occurred because of a personality clash between respondent and interviewer, for example, in the case of an elderly woman who was nervous about being interviewed by a young male interviewer. In this case the controller may want to reassign a callback/conversion attempt to another interviewer.

Completion

With PAPI telephone surveys, once an interview has been completed the call-sheet should be assigned a unique completion disposition code and then stapled to the completed questionnaire. After the questionnaire has been edited for completeness and any open-ended coding has been performed, a unique questionnaire identification number should be recorded on the call-sheet. In Figure 3.1, for example, a space is provided for this in the upper right corner of the call-sheet.

Occasionally when telephone numbers on call-sheets attached to completed interviews are called again (e.g., to verify the completion as discussed in Chapter 6), no one at the number claims any knowledge of the interview. Although some of these instances may be due to households not wanting to cooperate with the verification effort, in others it is due to carelessness on the part of the original interviewer; that is, occasionally an interviewer in a PAPI survey will mark the wrong call-sheet as a completion and attach it to a completed questionnaire in error. As discussed in Chapter 5, these problems are minimized when interviewers have adequate and well-organized space in which to work.

Simplifying the Call-Sheet

For many surveys, especially those conducted by students, the use of a professional style call-sheet, as shown in Figure 3.1, is overkill. If a group of interviewers will do only one telephone survey, and one with a relatively short field period (e.g., a week or less), it needlessly complicates matters to expect them to use an abstract set of numerical disposition codes.

Instead, a call-sheet similar to that presented in Figure 3.2 should be adequate. With a simplified call-sheet, temporary interviewers are expected to write only a brief note to the controller, explaining what happened with each dialing. Instead of listing a numerical disposition code for each outcome, they write messages such as, "no answer," "busy," "out of service," "refused," and so on. Although this makes it somewhat more time-consuming for the sampling pool controller (often the professor) to sort call-sheets after each session, and the historical information regarding the date and time of each dialing is lost, this simplified version works well enough for the needs of the typical class-related survey.

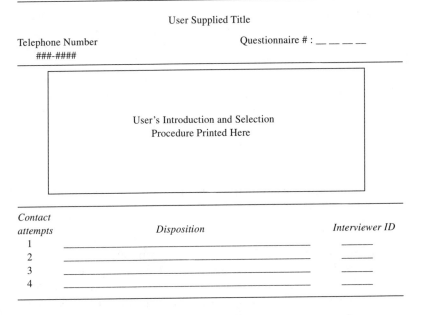

User Supplied Title

Telephone Number   Questionnaire # : __ __ __ __
###-####

User's Introduction and Selection
Procedure Printed Here

Contact attempts	Disposition	Interviewer ID
1		
2		
3		
4		

Figure 3.2. Example of a Simplified Call-Sheet.

Summary

At the end of the survey's field period, the controller ideally will have released the minimum amount of telephone numbers from the sampling pool needed to reach the survey's desired amount of completions. With dispositions such as nonworking, businesses, completions, and language barriers the controller stops processing the call-sheets as soon as any of these outcomes occur. New call-sheets are introduced on a limited basis in order to keep interviewer productivity at an acceptable rate, given the time within which the data must be gathered, but in a way that minimizes the number of noncontacts that remain unresolved when the desired sample size has been achieved.

Telephone numbers for which contact has been made and yet the designated respondent has not been interviewed and those that have continually rung but have never been answered can add to nonresponse error. In most surveys, it is impractical to process all call-sheets until a completion or other final disposition has been reached. Thus, it is the controller's responsibility to keep the number of call-sheets that remain in limbo at the end of the field period to a minimum. The number that remain in an unresolved condition at the end of the field period will depend in part on the number of callbacks budgeted. From the controller's standpoint, the goal is for each telephone number released from the sampling pool to be dialed the appropriate number of times allotted on the call-sheet.

A final comment: The use of a separate call-sheet for each telephone number should be viewed as a necessary, but not a sufficient condition for reducing potential nonresponse error. The more professional the attention given to controlling the sampling pool, the more likely this level of quality will carry over to all aspects of the telephone survey process.

REFUSAL REPORT FORM, REFUSAL CONVERSIONS, AND NONRESPONSE ERROR

Overall, a larger proportion of nonresponse in telephone surveys is due to refusals rather than to noncontacts as is the case in personal surveys (Groves & Lyberg, 1988). Furthermore, due in part to a small, but apparently constant increase in nonresponse rates over the past two decades, procedures have been developed and tested to lessen the potential problems refusals may cause (see Lyberg & Dean, 1992). One approach is the use of a structured form which interviewers complete after they encounter a refusal—a refusal report form (RRF). This form can provide information which may help the controller and interviewers in subsequent efforts to convert refusals and may help the surveyor learn more about the nature of potential nonresponse error.

Although somewhat counterintuitive, Groves (1989, pp. 218) is correct in warning that efforts to reduce nonresponse through refusal conversions (and extra callbacks in the case of noncontacts) could backfire, in some cases, by actually *increasing* nonresponse error and other survey error, such as measurement error. For example, if the quality of the data that are gathered from converted respondents is inferior to that gathered from other respondents, a survey's measurement error may increase to an extent that offsets any improvement in response rates (see Blair & Chun, 1992). Unfortunately, it is not always easy to determine when this might occur. Detailed consideration of these issues is complex and beyond the scope of this book; the advanced reader is referred to Groves (1989, pp. 133-238).

If a surveyor chooses to incorporate an RRF into the sampling process, it is not entirely obvious what information should be recorded; that is, as of 1992, use of these forms had not received much attention in the survey methods literature. With this in mind, the interested reader is urged to consider the following discussion of RRFs as suggestive and to follow the future literature.

Figure 3.3 is an example of an RRF used by NUSL; a form such as this could be used in PAPI or CATI surveys. The RRF is completed by an interviewer immediately after encountering a refusal (or refusal-partial). Using this RRF, the interviewer would begin by indicating *who* it was within a household who refused. This is not always obvious and depends upon information the interviewer gleans prior to the termination of the call. If an interviewer has not completed the respondent selection sequence (see Chapter 4) at the time of the refusal, the RRF should indicate that it was a household refusal. (An exception to this might be a survey in which one adult is selected as the respondent within a household and the interviewer has learned that the person refusing is the only adult in the household even though the formal selection procedure was not invoked.)

The interviewer might also code some basic demographics about the person refusing, but only if the interviewer has some degree of certainty in doing so. Preliminary research suggests that interviewers can do this accurately in a majority of cases for gender, age, and race (Bauman, Merkle, & Lavrakas, 1992; Lavrakas et al., 1992), although this deserves much more study before a final judgment is rendered on the validity of this approach. To the extent that this demographic information is accurate, it could be used by the controller to make decisions about which interviewers should attempt which refusal conversions and could be used by the surveyor to investigate potential nonresponse error associated with refusals. For example, preliminary findings suggest that interviewers of the same race as the person who initially refused will have better success in converting refusals. Furthermore, to the extent that demographic characteristics correlate with survey measures, the surveyor could investigate the effects of nonresponse by considering the demographic characteristics of the unconverted refusals; however, much more needs to be learned before the validity of this strategy is known.

Interviewers can also make ratings about the strength (severity) of the refusal (see Figure 3.3), as well as adding written comments and answering other questions that help to explain the exact nature of the verbal exchange (if any) that transpired prior to the termination of the call. Interviewers might also suggest their own ideas about what strategy could be employed in a conversion attempt.

The surveyor should determine the decision-rules that will be followed in choosing which initial refusals will be attempted for conversion and by whom. For example, in refusal conversion efforts at NUSL there is no recontact of households that have told the interviewer, "Don't call back!"

User Supplied Title

Interviewer #: _____

1. Did the person who refused have the last (most recent) birthday?
   Yes 35
   No/Uncertain 15

2. Demographics of the person refusing:

GENDER	AGE	RACE
Female 1	Child 0	Asian 1
Male 2	Adult < 30 1	Black 2
Uncertain 9	30-59 Yrs 2	Hispanic 3
	60 or Older 3	White 4
	Uncertain 9	Uncertain 9

3. Reason for refusal: _____

---

4. Strength of refusal: VERY WEAK 1 2 3 4 5 6 7 VERY STRONG
   Respondent attitude: VERY POLITE 1 2 3 4 5 6 7 VERY RUDE
                    NOT AT ALL ANGRY 1 2 3 4 5 6 7 VERY ANGRY

5. Did you tell the person:

		YES	NO
A.	How he or she was sampled?	1	2
B.	The nature/purpose of survey beyond the *standard* intro?	1	2
C.	Confidentiality?	1	2
D.	How the data would be used?	1	2
E.	Verification with supervisor/sponsor? . .	1	2

6. What can you recommend, if anything, for gaining respondent/household cooperation if a conversion attempt were made?

   _____
   _____
   _____

{PLEASE STAPLE TO CALL-SHEET AND RETURN TO SUPERVISOR}

Figure 3.3. Example of a Refusal Report Form (RRF).

or something explicit to that effect, as part of the initial refusal. At NUSL it is believed that this request should be respected. But short of that, conversions will be attempted with other initial refusals with the exception of those that are judged by the controller as being so hostile that prudence suggests not doing so; these very strong refusals appear to represent approximately 10%-15% of initial refusals. Of note, Groves and Lyberg (1988) recommend more discussion among survey researchers about the ethics of making conversion attempts.

In deciding which interviewer(s) should attempt conversions, several considerations can be kept in mind. First, very capable interviewers who see this as a welcome challenge are preferred. Second, as noted above, an interviewer's own gender, age, and race may be considered for particular conversion attempts. Furthermore, other preliminary findings suggest that initial refusals which occurred in daytime hours are somewhat more likely to be converted, as are those in which there is a relatively greater number of attempts at recontact between the initial refusal and the final conversion contact, and those in which the reason for the initial refusal was not explicitly linked to a lack of interest in the survey topic area (Lavrakas et al., 1992). The reader is reminded that these recommendations are suggestive and will await careful testing before they should be taken as certain advice.

No definitive evidence exists about the success rate of refusal conversion attempts, although Groves and Lyberg (1988) cite it in the 25%-40% range. In RDD general population surveys, with questionnaires that last 20-30 minutes, NUSL's success at conversions is typically in the 25%-30% range. Blair and Chun (1992) report success at the University of Maryland in the 25%-35% range. Frey (1989) cites success rates of about 40%, which is similar to rates cited by Alexander, Sebold, and Pfaff (1986). However, Collins et al. (1988) reported conversion rates in Great Britain of less than 20%.

In making decisions about whether or not to convert refusals, the surveyor is faced with this trade-off: Will resources be better spent on converting refusals to possibly decrease potential nonresponse error versus the possible increase in other potential sources of survey error that otherwise might be reduced if those same resources were invested differently (e.g., paying more to have better quality interviewers)?

EXPECTATIONS IN PROCESSING SAMPLING POOLS

It is helpful for surveyors, supervisory personnel, and interviewers to have realistic expectations about the relative proportion of the various call-sheet dispositions they can expect to encounter. Otherwise, they may become easily frustrated when they find that most dialings do not lead to completed interviews. Furthermore, the sampling pool controller must know what to expect in order to detect and resolve a potential problem before it leads to a possible increase in nonresponse and/or noncoverage errors.

The specific distribution of call-sheet dispositions in any given survey will depend a good deal on the efficiency of the sampling pool in reaching eligible respondents. For example, RDD sampling pools that have been stratified by prefix according to the proportion of working telephone numbers in the sampling area associated with each prefix and according to ranges of operating suffixes within each prefix (as discussed in Chapter 2) will contain far fewer nonworking numbers than a simple (unstratified) RDD sampling pool. The same advantage occurs with Mitofsky-Waksberg two-stage RDD sampling pools. The disposition of numbers released from a sampling pool generated from a list or a directory is likely to differ from that which results with RDD sampling. Also, every geographic area that is surveyed is likely to have its own idiosyncratic distribution of call-sheet dispositions.

Number of Dialings
Required to Complete a Survey

Chapter 2 discussed the size of the sampling pool that should be generated for a particular survey. This quantity is by no means the same as the number of *dialings* that interviewers can expect to make to reach the final sample size the surveyor desires. For example, interviewers for Groves and Kahn (1979) in their seminal study of (one-stage) RDD sampling of the continental United States made over 44,000 dialings (i.e., dispositions) in the process of using nearly 13,000 telephone numbers (i.e., call-sheets) in order to complete 1,700 interviews.

For an in-depth understanding of the dialing that is required of interviewers, let us look at a national two-stage RDD sampling pool processed in 1992 by NUSL. Nearly 4,600 telephone numbers were released in the process of reaching approximately 2,400 households and completing 1,500 interviews. Table 3.2 shows the outcome of the nearly 18,000 dialings that were made during the six-week field period. As is the case in probably all RDD surveys, the most frequent outcome was a ring-no-answer, which accounted for a third of all dialings (34%). Other frequent outcomes included: residential answering machines (22%); reaching a household but not the selected respondent (14%); completed interviews (8%); nonworking numbers (8%); and household refusals (5%; refusal conversions were attempted in this survey). Table 3.2 also illustrates the relative rarity of dialings that result in dispositions such as nonresidences, respondent refusals, partial interviews, and language barriers.

Another way of understanding the nature and magnitude of the sampling process is to consider how many call-sheets reach their final dispo-

Table 3.2

Disposition of Dialings ($N = 17,962$) in 1992 Two-Stage RDD Sampling of
United States

Disposition	Percentage of all dialings
Nonworking	8.0
Nonresidential	3.8
Never answered (no answering machine)	34.0
No adult resident	0.1
Non-English household/respondent	0.7
Residential answering machine	22.0
Household refusal	4.6
Answered, but selected respondent not reached	14.2
Selected respondent refusal	1.9
Partial	1.9
Mental/physical disability	0.4
Completed interview	8.4

SOURCE: Northwestern University Survey Laboratory, 1992.

sition after one, two, three, and more dialings. Table 3.3 presents these results for the 1992 national survey. Note that 2,158 (or 47%) of the 4,579 call-sheets reached their final disposition with *only one* dialing. However, if one were to eliminate the call-sheets that required only one dialing, it took an average of seven dialings to process each of the other 2,421 numbers. The total amount of dialing to process this sampling pool is considerably more than what would have been required of a similar survey a decade ago—the difference due primarily to residential answering machines and other harder-to-reach respondents.

Table 3.3 also illustrates a further aspect of the sampling process: the number of dialings that were required to complete specific interviews. Of the 1,500 completions, a fourth (27%) were completed on the first dialing and another fifth (21%) were completed on the second dialing. Thus, nearly half of the completions were attained with only one or two calls. Had this survey stopped processing call-sheets after three call-attempts (as is the case with many market research surveys), nearly 40% of the completions that were eventually attained would have been missed. If the survey had made no more than five dialings to any number nearly a fourth of the total completions would have been missed. However, processing call-sheets more than 10 times yielded less than 10% of the total completions.

Using the information shown in Table 3.3, one can calculate that of the nearly 18,000 dialings, one in six (16%) were the 10th, 11th, 12th, or more

Table 3.3
Number of Dialings for Final Disposition of All Call-Sheets (*N* = 4,579) and of All Completions (1,500)

Number of dialings	All call-sheets			Completions		
	Frequency	*Percentage*	*Cumulative percentage*	*Frequency*	*Percentage*	*Cumulative percentage*
1	2158	47.1	47.1	408	27.2	27.2
2	609	13.3	60.4	307	20.5	47.7
3	386	8.4	68.9	196	13.1	60.8
4	240	5.2	74.1	180	8.6	69.4
5	210	4.6	78.7	117	7.8	77.2
6	150	3.3	82.0	69	4.6	81.8
7	114	2.5	84.5	59	4.0	85.7
8	90	2.0	86.4	42	2.8	88.5
9	74	1.6	88.0	39	2.6	91.2
10-14	304	6.7	94.7	84	5.6	96.8
15-19	113	2.5	97.2	37	2.5	99.3
20-24	104	2.3	99.5	6	0.4	99.7
25 or more	25	0.5	100.0	5	0.3	100.0
TOTALS	4579	100.0		1500	100.0	

SOURCE: Northwestern University Survey Laboratory, 1992.

dialing. From the perspective of total survey error, one can question whether the expense associated with this significant effort (i.e., placing 2,863 additional dialings beyond nine attempts) was worth the 132 completions (i.e., 9% of the total 1,500 completions) it yielded. That is, could the resources associated with this increase in sample size (thereby slightly reducing sampling error) have been of greater benefit if committed to trying to reduce some other aspect(s) of total survey error?

**Distribution of Final Dispositions
in an RDD Sample**

Table 3.4 shows the final disposition of each call-sheet used in the 1992 RDD survey—that is, the status at the end of the field period of each call-sheet released from the sampling pool. In the process of making the 17,962 dialings reported above, 4,579 telephone numbers were used. As a testimony to the efficiency of the two-stage RDD process, more than half of the numbers reached a household, with the most frequent final disposition being a completed interview (33%). Other final dispositions that frequently occurred were nonworking numbers (29%), nonresidential numbers (15%), and, as a group, refusals and partials (13%). From the standpoint of noncontacts and, thus, potential nonresponse error, a relatively small proportion of all the processed numbers ended with either the respondent never being available (2%)—which includes some with residential answering machines —or numbers that were never answered (4%), most of which are unlikely to be residences (see Groves & Lyberg, 1988, p. 199).

Another RDD Example

Findings from another relatively large RDD survey conducted in the Chicago metropolitan area in 1991, using one-stage RDD stratified by prefix and cleaned of vacuous suffixes (see Chapter 2), reinforces the pattern of final dispositions found in the 1992 national survey. Interviewing for the 1991 survey was done by NUSL, which processed 3,005 call-sheets in completing 1,027 interviews.

Table 3.5 shows the final dispositions of all call-sheets used in the 1991 Chicago area survey. Similar to the 1992 national survey (see Table 3.4), completed interviews accounted for one third (34%) of all those released from the sampling pool. Nonworking (21%), nonresidential (16%), and refusals or partials (17%) were other frequently experienced final dispositions. Again, a relatively small proportion of all the processed numbers

Table 3.4

Final Disposition of Call-Sheets ($N = 4,579$) in 1992 Two-Stage RDD
Sampling of United States

Final disposition	Percentage of all numbers processed
Nonworking	29.1
Nonresidential	14.8
Never answered (no answering machine)	4.0
No adult resident	0.5
Non-English household/respondent	2.3
Residential answering machine, never answered	1.0
Household refusal	6.6
Selected respondent never reached	2.1
Selected respondent refusal	4.6
Partial	1.5
Mental/physical disability	1.0
Completed interview	32.8

SOURCE: Northwestern University Survey Laboratory, 1991.

ended as either a respondent noncontact (3%) or were numbers that were never answered (3%).

In sum, the scope of the work facing the controller and the interviewing staff in RDD sampling will depend upon the geographic area for a particular survey and on the manner in which the sampling pool was generated. If full information about each prefix in the sampling area is employed or a two-stage approach is used in generating the sampling pool, one can anticipate well over a 50% reduction in the number of call-sheets that will be processed compared with simple (unstratified) RDD sampling.

List-Based Sampling Pool

If a sampling pool is generated from a list or directory, far fewer call-sheets are likely to be processed to achieve the desired number of completions compared with what is required in an RDD survey. Yet even with up-to-date lists, it is not unusual for 50%-100% more call-sheets to be needed for processing than the total number of completions planned. Thus, for example, a survey for which 400 completions are planned may require a sampling pool of 600 or more telephone numbers to be processed.

The following example is typical of my experience with surveys of special populations using a list-based sampling frame/pool. In this case a national survey of law enforcement chief executives (i.e., police chiefs

Table 3.5

Final Disposition of Call-Sheets (N = 3,005) in 1991 Chicago Metropolitan Area Stratified RDD Sampling

Final disposition	Number	Percentage of all sample numbers
Nonworking	636	21.2
Nonresidential	478	15.9
Residence outside sampling area	78	2.6
Never answered (no answering machine)	78	2.6
Non-English household/respondent	98	3.3
Residential answering machine, never answered	15	0.5
Household refusal	302	10.0
Selected respondent never reached	69	2.3
Selected respondent refusal	150	5.0
Partial	28	1.9
Mental/physical disability	39	1.3
Completed interviews	1,027	34.2
Miscellaneous other	7	0.2

SOURCE: Northwestern University Survey Laboratory, 1991.

and sheriffs) was conducted in 1988 by NUSL. The sampling pool was randomly generated from a data base created by the Bureau of the Census of all law enforcement agencies in the United States (see Lavrakas & Rosenbaum, 1989). As shown in Table 3.6, telephone numbers for 1,117 agencies were released from the sampling pool in the course of completing 788 interviews. (Advance letters were sent to each of the 1,117 executives prior to placing telephone calls; see Chapter 4.) In contrast to RDD surveys of the public, twice the proportion of final dispositions resulted in completions (71%). Unlike RDD surveys, relatively more of the nonresponse was associated with noncontact (16%) than was due to refusals (6%). (Despite what some may assume, special populations are quite likely to participate in a well-executed telephone survey that is relevant to their own profession and that plans callbacks at the convenience of the respondent.)

Panel Studies

What can a surveyor and sampling pool controller expect with telephone panel studies, which reinterview respondents after some passage of time? My own experience shows that the success that interviewers have

Table 3.6

Final Disposition of Call-Sheets ($N = 1,117$)
in 1988 National Law Enforcement Chief Executives Sampling

Final of all sample disposition	Number	Percentage numbers
No correct telephone number	30	2.7
No law enforcement responsibility	39	3.5
No contact ever made	7	0.6
No CEO appointed	9	0.8
Department refusal	22	2.0
CEO never available	174	15.5
CEO refusal	41	3.7
Partial	3	0.2
Completed interviews	788	70.5
Miscellaneous other	4	0.4

SOURCE: Lavrakas and Rosenbaum (1989).

in reinterviewing an original respondent, in particular in an RDD study, will depend largely upon residential mobility patterns within the sampling area (see Lavrakas, Settersten, & Maier, 1991). In the large cities, about 50%-60% of original respondents can be found and reinterviewed after a one-year time lag; in suburban areas this figure may be as high as 70%-75%.

Of note, one need not know a respondent's name to reinterview her or him via telephone. Instead, success has been found to be comparable to what occurs when names are known in reinterviewing original respondents for whom their gender and age were known but not their names (see Lavrakas et al., 1991). Upwards of 90% of original respondents who can be reached at Wave 2 of a panel study can be successfully reinterviewed; the remainder refuse or are never available during the survey's field period.

Callbacks and Nonresponse

Telephone surveys of the public and of special populations will experience differing patterns of final dispositions depending on the number of callbacks that are planned/budgeted. In market research, three callback attempts are considered more than adequate by many surveyors. In contrast, academic-based surveys and most federal government-sponsored telephone surveys typically allow for 10 or 20 or even more callbacks (see Traugott, 1987). It should be obvious that the distribution of final dispositions will differ markedly in the former case (market research) versus the latter.

Our own multivariate analyses of callbacks in RDD surveys shows that those persons who are reached with only a few call-attempts are more likely to be female, less educated, unemployed, married, and older, and also are more likely to report to be in relatively poorer health (Merkle, Bauman, & Lavrakas, 1991). This profile is fairly consistent with other findings on easy-to-reach versus hard-to-reach respondents (see Groves & Lyberg, 1988). To the extent that factors such as these are related to the substantive focus of a survey there will almost certainly be nonresponse error (bias) in the findings of any survey that conducts relatively few callbacks. Whether this bias will be large or small is not often obvious and it remains the responsibility of the surveyor to make an a priori decision about the relative importance of the allocation of resources for multiple callbacks.

SAMPLING POOL DISPOSITIONS
AND SURVEY RESPONSE AND NONRESPONSE RATES

A major reason to employ a highly controlled system for processing sampling pools in telephone surveys is to achieve a reasonably high response rate within a given sampling area, with the potential of lessening the chance for nonresponse error. In CATI surveys that employ software to control the sampling pool, supervisory staff should be able to devote even more attention to the processing of especially challenging respondents/ households, thereby reducing nonresponse even further than in an otherwise comparable PAPI survey.

Although this section is not an exhaustive discussion of telephone survey response and nonresponse rates, it will illustrate some of the issues that should be considered whether one is preparing to report about a completed survey's methodology or whether one is evaluating the likely quality (validity) of another survey. Currently most survey professionals agree that response rates are best considered as a range rather than as a single value. In general, response rates are affected by the survey topic, the length of the questionnaire, the caliber of the organization and interviewing staff that is conducting the survey, the length of the field period, rules for callbacks and refusal conversions, and other factors. Furthermore, Groves (1989, p. 133) warns that these rates, in themselves, are not a direct measure of nonresponse error, the latter being a function of the response/nonresponse rate and whatever differences may exist between those who responded and those who did not on the variables a survey is trying to measure. For those seeking additional discussion of these issues, see Fowler (1993), Frey (1989), and Groves and Lyberg (1988).

For purposes of illustration in this chapter, results from the 1991 Chicago metropolitan RDD survey and the 1992 national RDD survey discussed earlier will be used. Referring to Tables 3.4 and 3.5, one can see the distribution of all call-sheets (i.e., telephone numbers) used in those surveys.

Sampling Pool Efficiency Rates

Table 3.7 shows various response rates associated with these surveys. Different response rates can be calculated depending on what is used as the numerator and denominator (see Groves, 1989; Kviz, 1977; Traugott, Groves, & Lepkowski, 1987). For example, a measure for the efficiency of the sampling pool in reaching working numbers for the 1992 national RDD survey is 71% (i.e., 3246/4579 = .709); thus, only 1,333 numbers, or 29%, released from the sampling pool were confirmed as nonworking. In this respect the sampling pool was very efficient, confirming the appeal of the Mitofsky-Waksberg two-stage approach. The 1991 local survey's efficiency was even higher (79%), confirming the value of stratifying by prefix and cleaning for vacuous suffix ranges in local RDD surveys (when this approach is feasible).

As a measure of the efficiency of the 1992 sampling pool in reaching residential households, a conservative estimate would be to subtract the 676 call-sheets that reached nonresidential numbers from the numerator, but to leave in the 184 call-sheets that were never answered after 30+ dialings. This would yield 2670/4579, or 56%. However, in all likelihood, nearly all of these never-answered numbers were not residential. The field period for this survey extended for seven weeks, during which time each of these numbers was tried 30 or more times on various days of the week and weekend and at various times of the day and evening. Thus it is reasonable to assume that most rang at coin telephones, in warehouses or other nonresidential locations, or were not in operation. Following this reasoning, these 184 call-sheets could be subtracted from the numerator, yielding a more conservative rate of 52% for the efficiency of the sampling pool in reaching residential numbers within this sampling area. The comparable rate for the 1991 survey is 60%.

Completion Rates

To calculate a gross completion rate for the 1992 survey, one could compare the 1,500 completions to the entire set of 4,579 call-sheets used.

Table 3.7

Completion Rate Calculations for 1991 and 1992 Surveys

| Type of rate | Comparison | 1991 Local RDD | | 1992 National RDD | |
		Numerator/Denominator	Rate	Numerator/Denominator	Rate
Gross efficiency of sampling pool	Working numbers/All numbers	2369/3005	78.8%	3246/4579	70.9%
Efficiency of sampling pool in reaching households	Possible households/All numbers	1891/3005	62.9%	2570/4579	56.1%
Conservative estimate of efficiency of sampling pool in reaching houseolds	Probable households/All numbers	1813/3005	60.3%	2386/4579	52.1%
Gross completion rate	All completions/All numbers	1027/3005	34.2%	1500/4579	32.8%
Conservative completion rate	All completions/All possible households	1027/1891	54.3%	1500/2570	58.4%
Most reasonable completion rate	All completions/All eligibles	1027/1598	64.3%	1500/2216	67.7%

SOURCE: Northwestern University Survey Laboratory, 1991 and 1992.

As shown in Table 3.7, this yields a rate of about 33%. For the 1991 survey, a nearly identical gross completion rate is found (34%; 1027/3005).

A more telling estimate of the success of the 1992 survey in completing interviews at residential numbers would be to use all possible household numbers (including never-answered numbers) in the denominator. This yields a ratio of 1500/2570 or 58%. For the 1991 survey, a slightly lower rate is found (54%; 1027/1891).

A more reasonable completion rate would eliminate from the denominator those numbers that can be argued to be ineligible. In these surveys, this would include households in which no one met the age requirements, households in which the household or designated respondent could not speak English or was permanently physically/mentally incapable of participating, and numbers that were never answered after a very large number of call-attempts. Using this reasoning, two out of every three eligible respondents (68%; 1500/2216) in the 1992 national survey were successfully interviewed, compared with a slightly lower proportion (64%; 1027/1598) in the 1991 local survey.

Overall, what comparisons can be made about the processing of the sampling pools in these two surveys? On the one hand, the method used to generate the 1991 local survey was somewhat more efficient in reaching eligible households than that used in the 1992 national survey, although the respective methods were the best approaches for each particular survey. On the other hand, the success in completing interviews at households, thereby lessening nonresponse, was somewhat better in the 1992 study. (Of note, the average caliber of interviewers employed on the 1992 study was slightly higher than for the 1991 study, which may have contributed to the lower level of nonresponse in the 1992 study.) Finally, each survey used refusal conversion attempts with 27% and 25% being converted in the 1991 and 1992 surveys, respectively.

Rates of Nonresponse

Other rates that are often calculated have to do with the nature of the nonresponse. Table 3.8 shows a detailed breakdown of the dispositions that reached (or possibly reached) households that did not lead to completed interviews for the 1991 and 1992 surveys. By far, the largest proportion of nonresponse in each survey was due to refusals, which is the common pattern in telephone surveys of the general public (Groves & Lyberg, 1988). In each survey more of the refusals came from a person in the household other than the selected respondent or occurred prior to a respondent being selected. In each survey about 1 in 10 cases of nonresponse was due to language barriers and to the selected respondent never being available at the time a dialing was attempted. In the 1992 national survey, nearly twice the proportion of nonresponse was due to numbers that were never answered, compared with the 1991 survey. Finally, it is worth noting that in each survey, there was only a very small proportion of the nonresponse in which a residential answering machine was the culprit.

Refusal/completion rates for these surveys, which might be labeled the *noncooperation rate* (see Groves & Lyberg, 1988, p. 200), can be calculated by comparing the number of completions with the number of call-sheets that ended in some form of refusal (i.e., household refusals, respondent refusals, and partials). For the 1991 survey, using 1,507 (1027 + 480) as the denominator and 480 (all forms of refusals) as the numerator, the noncooperation rate was approximately 32%. For the 1992 survey it was about 28%.

It should be remembered that nonresponse rates for a sample are only one form of survey nonresponse. In addition to the topics discussed in this section, there is the issue of *item* nonresponse (i.e., missing answers to a particular questionnaire item). Fortunately, with capable telephone interviewers using well-developed survey instruments, item nonresponse is not likely to contribute in any appreciable way to total survey error for the vast majority of questionnaire items.

Weighting to Adjust for Nonresponse

A common practice, although not always an adequate or even a valid one, is to perform postsampling statistical adjustments (weighting) in an attempt to partially compensate for possible nonresponse error (see Henry, 1990). This is done typically by adjusting for variations in the sample's demographic characteristics compared with the same characteristics in the target population (usually derived from census data). For example, the sample may be composed of 40% male, whereas the adult population may be 46% male. In this case each male respondent would receive a gender-weight of 46/40, or 1.15 (i.e., each male would be treated as 1.15 respondents and each female, in turn, would be treated as 54/60, or 0.9, respondents). The validity of these postsampling adjustments rests on the oftentimes unsubstantiated assumption that those persons, who are "up-weighted" to compensate for missing respondents of similar demographic characteristics, provided data that is similar to what would have been gathered from these demographically similar, but "missing," others. For

Table 3.8

Reasons for Nonresponse[a] for 1991 (N = 779) and 1992 (N = 1,049) Surveys

Source of nonresponse	Percentage of noncompletions	
	1991 Survey	1992 Survey
Never answered (no answering machine)	10.0	17.5
Non-English-speaking household/respondent	12.6	9.9
Selected respondent never reached	8.9	9.1
Selected respondent refused	19.2	19.7
Breakoff of interview	3.6	6.7
Residential answering machine, never answered	1.9	4.2
Respondent with mental/physical disability	5.0	4.3
Household respondent refused	38.8	28.6

SOURCE: Northwestern University Survey Laboratory, 1991 and 1992.
a. These are the dispositions of the last calls made to households for which no completed interviews were secured.

an advanced discussion of these issues, the interested reader is urged to study Groves (1989, pp. 156-188).

Of note, statistical weighting to compensate for nonresponse is different from the postsampling weighting that is routinely and appropriately performed to adjust for unequal probabilities of selection, for example, in RDD surveys in which some households have a greater chance of being sampled due to multiple residential telephone numbers.

Summary

At the end of the field period there are a variety of ways to measure the quality of the sampling process. It is good practice to calculate response and nonresponse rates to provide information regarding the relative success of the survey in reaching a representative sample within the target population. Those publishing the results of their surveys are encouraged to report many of these rates and to explicitly discuss the potential effects of noncoverage and nonresponse on survey findings so that others can readily assess the relative quality of the sampling that occurred.

SAMPLING POOLS IN MIXED MODE SURVEYS

With the increasing use of mixed mode surveys (see Dillman & Tarnai, 1988; Traugott et al., 1987), in part to counter the somewhat declining response rates many surveys are experiencing, a surveyor may encounter a situation in which part of the sampling pool is processed by telephone, part by mail, and/or part via personal interviewing. These surveys require that addresses are known for the portion of the sampling pool that is processed by mail or in person; the addresses may be contained in the initial sampling frame or may be gathered via preliminary telephone screening. An exception would be "mailing" a questionnaire via a fax telephone number, in which case the respondent's address need not be known.

Of note, there has been a small but increasing trend in the past decade for selected respondents to refuse to do the interview via telephone but to tell the interviewer they would be willing to participate if the questionnaire were mailed to them. It is my experience that many of these exchanges come from older adults who have been warned by senior citizen magazines to be suspicious of telephone surveys. Unfortunately, accommodating these requests usually is not as simple as getting an address and mailing the questionnaire out. For instance, the format of the telephone instrument, especially if it is on CATI, is rarely appropriate for self-administration; thus, it often is not practical to change to a mixed mode approach once a study has begun.

A special advantage of mixed mode surveys that are *planned* to employ a mixed mode approach is that they provide the ability to send advance letters (see Chapter 4) to alert respondents of the forthcoming survey and to help establish credibility for the survey endeavor. With surveys of business-based respondents, advance letters can be sent via fax, assuming the fax number is known or has been gathered via a preliminary telephone contact.

An example of a sampling pool NUSL processed via mail, telephone, and in person will help to illustrate what might be encountered in a mixed mode survey of the public. The survey was conducted in 1990 for a local school district (Morton Grove, Illinois) that wanted extremely precise measures on future enrollment (Lavrakas, 1990). The sample design required that approximately two thirds of the 3,000 households in the district be interviewed and that at least a 90% response rate be achieved. The initial sampling frame was composed of all addresses on the district's mailing list. This list was verified by checking approximately 10% of the addresses on the list with actual addresses on streets throughout the community. Through this process more addresses were identified. The list was further supplemented by using a reverse telephone directory; approximately 80% of the households had listed telephone numbers and thus listed addresses. A systematic random sampling pool of 2,210 addresses was then generated and a postcard was sent alerting each household of the forthcoming survey. Approximately one week later the two-page questionnaire was mailed with a stamped return envelope. After 10 additional days all households with listed telephone numbers that had not mailed back their questionnaire received a follow-up call, either as a reminder to send back the questionnaire or to actually complete the questionnaire via telephone. Households without listed telephone numbers were mailed a second questionnaire. A second set of follow-up telephone contacts also was conducted. Finally, all nonresponding households were contacted in person.

By the conclusion of the eight-week field period during which time this mixed mode sampling pool was processed, a 92% response rate was attained: 66% responded via mail; 15% via telephone; and 11% through in-person interviews. (From the standpoint of potential nonresponse error associated with the 8% of the sampling pool that were not successfully interviewed, there was good evidence to believe that those households not responding were composed mostly of elderly residents and others without school-aged children.)

This mixed mode survey used telephoning to great advantage, both to encourage compliance with the mail questionnaire and to conduct a sixth of the completions. From a cost/benefit standpoint, the mixed mode survey cost about the same as what an exclusively telephone-based survey would have cost, although the field period lasted about twice as long. However, offsetting the disadvantage of a longer field period, the mixed mode approach very likely had considerably less noncoverage and nonresponse error than would have been the case if only telephone interviewing had been conducted.

Unfortunately, the conditions that favored success in this mixed mode school district study—in particular a very short questionnaire on a topic of high salience to respondents—are not often present. However, because of the advantages that mixed mode surveys may afford, surveyors should be alert constantly to opportunities in which the mixed mode approach should be deployed.

PROCESSING SAMPLING POOLS WITH CATI

As noted earlier, not all CATI environments employ computer control of the sampling pool; that is, in some cases CATI is used only to administer the questionnaire, and the sampling pool is still processed manually with paper-and-pencil call-sheets. However, with CATI systems that control the sampling pool the supervisory staff should have considerably more information with which to make informed decisions about the sampling process. For example, daily reports can be generated easily to detail the exact status of the portion of the sampling pool that has been released. The software might generate the sampling pool, one number at a time, as it is needed by the next interviewer. The software may be used also to schedule callbacks at specific times when an appointment has been made or at different times/days for never-answered numbers.

The appeal of all these advantages notwithstanding, I believe the greatest attraction of CATI, as it relates to sampling, is that it releases resources that are required in PAPI telephone surveys for supervisory staff to manually process the sampling pool. These resources can then be used for supervisory staff to spend more time making decisions about the sample and to monitor interviewers more intensely (see Chapter 6). In this way, noncoverage error, nonresponse error, and measurement error may be reduced thereby lowering total survey error.

EXERCISES

Exercise 3.1: Using the dispositions shown in Table 3.1 as an example, develop a category system that would have interviewers use 10 or fewer disposition codes. Explain your reasoning for collapsing categories.

Exercise 3.2: Compose the text of a standardized spiel for interviewers to leave on residential answering machines. Keep it to about 50 words or less.

Exercise 3.3: Write two scenarios of the dialogue that might be experienced by a telephone interviewer that demonstrate your understanding of the difference between a household refusal and a respondent refusal.

Exercise 3.4: Calculate each of the response rates shown in Table 3.7 using data given to you by your professor.

Exercise 3.5: Prepare a table of noncompletions as shown in Table 3.8 using the data given to you by your professor.

4

Selecting Respondents and Securing Cooperation

Some persons unfamiliar with valid telephone survey methods erroneously assume that the first person who answers the telephone is the one who is interviewed. This is not the case with any survey designed to gather a representative *within-unit* sample of a target population (e.g., adults within households) and thereby have a decreased likelihood of noncoverage error. For example, although males and females are born at a near 50:50 rate, the adult population in most urban communities is closer to a 55:45 female/male split. A survey that strives to conduct interviews with a representative sample of females and males must rely on a systematic respondent selection procedure to achieve this balance.

This chapter covers various issues concerning the representative selection of a respondent within a sampling unit, such as a household, and securing the cooperation of the selected respondent (thereby lessening nonresponse). The manner in which the survey is introduced when contact is first made with a household is often critical to overall compliance and particularly to the successful resolution of respondent selection. Therefore, the value of well-constructed introductory/selection spiels is explained also.

The chapter begins with a review of the importance of controlled (systematic) selection of respondents for telephone surveys. The following section addresses the importance of the introduction that interviewers use to establish rapport quickly at the point of contact. Included in this section is an explanation of the need to train interviewers to be prepared to respond with standard answers to common questions asked by respondents about the survey. After this, frequently employed respondent selection techniques are reviewed. The chapter concludes with a discussion of advance contact of survey respondents and its relationship to selection and securing cooperation.

STARTING OFF ON A SOLID FOOTING

With the plethora of sophisticated telephone equipment that has been developed in the age of the microchip it is no wonder that many people complain about being hounded by telephone calls from strangers. Telemarketing, some done entirely by machine, has become a cost-effective method for myriad businesses to sell their products or to get their messages across. It is this "real-world" environment in which serious telephone surveys must contend. The immediate challenge faced by a telephone survey interviewer when the telephone is answered is to convey adequate information in a manner that effectively differentiates the survey from a "junk call." It is the purpose of the introduction/selection sequence and the responsibility of the interviewer who uses it to accomplish this.

In contrast to in-person surveys, refusals to telephone surveys are much more likely to occur at the very beginning of interviewer contact rather than after a respondent has been selected or after the questionnaire has started (see Collins et al., 1988). Oksenberg and Cannell (1988) report that about 40% of refusals generally occur during the first few sentences of the introduction; another 50% occur later in the introduction/selection sequence; and 10% or fewer occur after the interviewer has started the questionnaire. Thus the first 30-60 seconds of contact are crucial ones, particularly from the standpoint of minimizing nonresponse.

How, then, does a surveyor balance two important agendas—minimizing noncoverage and nonresponse—that occur simultaneously at the beginning of interviewer-respondent contact? A surveyor typically wants to end the field period with as demographically representative a final sample as possible by avoiding the threats of noncoverage. However, techniques that are likely to choose the most representative demographic mixture of individuals within sampling units are also ones that take longest to employ and that are more likely to cause suspicion because of their intrusive nature, thereby increasing the chances of nonresponse.

The skill of interviewers does much to determine the success of any telephone survey in balancing these competing agendas. However, even excellent interviewers will have trouble if an introductory spiel is awkward or if the respondent selection method is worded in a confusing or threatening fashion. In contrast, even inexperienced interviewers can succeed if they are trained to properly use a well-worded introduction with a relatively nonintrusive and persuasive selection procedure.

Obviously, when sampling is done from a list and the respondent is a particular individual known by name, respondent selection requires merely that interviewers ask for that person. But in many instances with list sampling and with all RDD sampling, interviewers will not know the name of the person within a sampling unit (e.g., household) who should be interviewed. (An exception occurs when a designated respondent's name has been learned during an earlier call-attempt that did not lead to a completed interview.) Therefore, a survey designed to gather estimates of person-level population parameters (as opposed to household-level measures) must employ a systematic selection technique to maximize external validity (i.e., generalizability).

As mentioned earlier, surveys that interview merely the first person who answers the telephone and who sounds old enough to answer the questions are not likely to gather data that validly reflect the attitudes, behaviors, and experiences of the target population because noncoverage error *within* sampling units is likely to occur. Surveys that allow interviewers to speak with whomever they want within a sampling unit will also suffer from this problem. For example, imagine a survey in which interviewers spoke with the person in each sampling unit most willing to be interviewed at the time. This approach may please interviewers, but is likely to have disastrous consequences on the representativeness of the final sample. Therefore, respondents should be selected in a systematic and unbiased fashion, which means interviewers cannot choose for themselves the person within a sampling unit to interview.

Respondents can be selected within a sampling unit using a true probability sampling scheme, although surveyors will not always need or want to employ such a rigorous approach due to its highly intrusive nature. Rather, for the purposes of most surveys, it will be acceptable to use a technique that systematically balances selection along the lines of both gender and age. Because most sampling units (e.g., households) are homogeneous on many other demographic characteristics (e.g., race, education, and religion), representative sampling of units should provide adequate coverage of the population on these other demographic factors.

INTRODUCING THE SURVEY

There are differing opinions among survey professionals regarding how much information should be given in the spiel that is used to introduce the survey, and the research literature does not provide a definitive answer (see Groves & Lyberg, 1988, pp. 202-210). I side with those who believe it should be reasonably brief so that the respondent can be actively engaged via the start of the questionnaire. Exceptions to this rule exist, as in the case where an introduction must contain instructions regarding how the questionnaire is organized or about unusual types of questions. Furthermore, although the content of the spiel is important, how well interviewers deploy it may be even more important (see Chapter 5).

I recommend that an introductory spiel contain enough information to reduce as much as possible any nervousness on the part of the person answering the telephone who hears that a stranger is calling to conduct a telephone survey (see Frey, 1989, pp. 125-137). In other words, the credibility of the interviewer (and thus the survey) must be established as soon as possible, and it is the task of the introduction to do this.

At the same time, experience demonstrates that getting someone's full cooperation is easier once he or she begins the questionnaire—somewhat like the "foot-in-the-door" technique. The longer the introduction and the more a potential respondent must listen without active involvement, the greater the chance she or he will lose interest before questioning even begins (Dillman, Gallegos, & Frey, 1976). Whenever possible, and especially if a surveyor has any doubts, an introductory spiel should be pretested along with the rest of the selection method and the questionnaire itself.

Developing an Introductory Spiel

Although surveyors may differ in the exact way they prefer to word introductions, the following information is consistent with disclosure guidelines of the American Association for Public Opinion Research (AAPOR, 1991) and the National Council on Public Polls (Gawiser & Witt, 1992) and I recommend strongly that it be considered for inclusion:

1. identification of the interviewer, the interviewer's affiliation, and the survey's sponsor;
2. a brief explanation of the purpose of the survey and its sampling area (or target population);
3. some positively worded phrase to encourage cooperation; and
4. verification of the telephone number dialed by the interviewer.

Figure 4.1 is an example of an introduction/selection sheet with a typical introductory spiel used at NUSL. In some surveys it is necessary that a copy of this sheet be attached to every call-sheet released from the sampling pool, whereas in others only one copy needs to be placed at each interviewing station. The introductory statement in Figure 4.1 begins with the interviewer introducing herself or himself by name, identifying where the call is originating, and explaining why the call is being made. Included in the wording about the purpose of the call is a reference to the sampling area and the survey sponsor. Whenever possible, some implicit or explicit statement should be made about the use of the findings, unless that might confound the answers given by respondents. If the questionnaire is a short

---

INTRODUCTION/SELECTION SHEET: EVANSTON ANTICRIME SURVEY

Hello, my name is _____, and I'm calling from the Northwestern University Survey Laboratory. We are conducting a short random survey of Evanston residents in cooperation with the Evanston Police Department. The purpose of the survey is to determine how people feel about the safety and security of their neighborhoods, so that the city can plan better anticrime programs. (Your cooperation is voluntary, but we'd greatly appreciate your help.)

Before I continue, may I please verify that this is _____? **[VERIFY TELE-PHONE NUMBER]**

User Supplied Selection Procedure

Figure 4.1. Example of an Introductory Spiel.

one (say, under 10 minutes), I recommend mentioning its brevity in the introduction. If the interview will take 15 minutes or longer, I suggest that no statement be made about the time required, unless a respondent asks, "How long will it take?" In that case, all interviewers should be trained to give the same (honest) answer through use of a standardized *fallback* statement. (These statements are discussed in the next section.)

The introductory spiel also should include a verification of the telephone number the interviewer dialed to further professionalize the contact and to assist quality control of the processing of the sampling pool. In the first edition of this book I recommended that the number verification be performed immediately upon making contact (Lavrakas, 1987, p. 84). I have come to believe that this approach is an unnecessarily intrusive start, which many interviewers find difficult. By positioning it lower in the introductory spiel, some rapport has developed before it is asked. It is especially important that the number dialed is verified in RDD surveys both for sample control purposes and to avoid the problems call forwarding can create (e.g., call forwarding alters the probability of selection in unknown ways).

Fallback Statements

In most surveys it is unnecessary, and thus inadvisable, to devise an introductory spiel that contains a detailed explanation of what the survey is about. If the respondent wants to know more about the survey before making the decision to participate, interviewers should be given an honest, standardized explanation to read or paraphrase. For those respondents who seem reluctant to participate, interviewers should be trained to exercise discretion and possibly convey an even more detailed explanation of the survey's purpose.

There are a few basic types of information-seeking exchanges that are occasionally initiated with interviewers by prospective respondents (see Lavrakas & Merkle, 1991). The word *occasionally* is important to keep in mind: If interviewers were almost always asked these questions, then it would be wise to incorporate the information conveyed in the answers into the introductory spiel read to everyone. Preliminary research on this topic suggests that about one in three respondents asks interviewers some type of substantive question about the survey prior to the start of the interview (Lavrakas & Merkle, 1991). (Furthermore, there was a small but statistically significant trend for black interviewers to be asked more questions than white interviewers and for black respondents to ask more questions than white respondents. No other demographic patterns were found.)

However, since in the majority of cases interviewers will not need to provide a more lengthy explanation, it expedites matters by not reading the detailed information to everyone, thereby lessening the chance of nonresponse. The types of information that are sometimes asked include:

1. What is the purpose of the survey and how will the findings be used?
2. How did you get my telephone number?
3. Who is conducting/sponsoring this survey?
4. Why can't someone else in my household participate?

For each of these questions written fallback statements should be provided to interviewers to enable them to give honest, standardized answers to respondents who ask them. Figure 4.2 is an example of a typical fallback sheet (also see Frey, 1989, p. 230). In all cases the explanations should include a reminder that the answers to the questionnaire are confidential and the respondent's cooperation is voluntary, so as to be consistent with the spirit of "informed consent" (Frey, 1989, pp. 247-250).

C25 INTERVIEWER FALLBACK SHEET

Explanation of Survey: The survey is very short, about two or three minutes. Most of the questions deal with your opinions about heart transplant operations. It's important that we speak with people regardless of how much they think they know about these operations, so that we can get a true picture of attitudes throughout Chicago. I'm taking a course at Northwestern called "Advanced Reporting," and my class is conducting this survey as part of our course work. All your answers are confidential; your cooperation is voluntary, but I'd greatly appreciate your help.

Use of Survey: As part of my course, I have to write a news story for my professor about the results of this survey. As a class, we have to interview several hundred Chicago residents. All answers will be grouped together; no responses will be identified with any specific person. Your cooperation is voluntary, but I'd greatly appreciate your help.

Random Digit Dialing: Your number was chosen by a technique called *random digit dialing.* My professor put all the 3-digit telephone exchanges that ring in Chicago into a computer, and the computer randomly added 4 more digits to make up 7-digit phone numbers. . . . That's how we reached your home. . . . We use this technique because it's important that we speak with people throughout the City of Chicago, regardless whether their numbers are listed or unlisted. That's the only way we can get a survey that will *fairly* represent the opinions of Chicago residents.

Female/Male Selection: I have a sheet here that tells me the one person in your home whom I can interview. Sometimes it picks the oldest or youngest woman to be interviewed, while other times it picks the oldest or youngest man. This is the only way we will get a fair balance of younger and older females and males.

Check-up: If you have any questions about this survey, you can contact my professor, Dr. Lavrakas, at 491-5662 during the daytime.

Figure 4.2. Example of Fallback Statements.

The goal of fallback statements is to help the interviewer convince the potential respondent that the survey is a worthwhile (and harmless) endeavor. This should be kept in mind by the person who composes the statements.

Incentives to Participate

In constructing an introductory spiel, fallback statements, and the wording of any respondent selection sequence, it behooves a surveyor to think of the incentives (and disincentives) that respondents may have for participation (see also Chapter 5). The interested reader is encouraged to seek out Groves (1989, pp. 215-236) for a detailed review of the pertinent social science literature.

Surveyors may, for example, consider providing a monetary incentive to survey respondents, although this can be difficult to implement in a telephone survey. Other material incentives, such as a chance to win a prize or offering to send a research report, may be considered. The research literature on the effects of material incentives is far from definitive and there are enough conflicting findings to encourage a surveyor to consider carefully their use (see Groves, 1989, pp. 215-217). If a material incentive is used, then its explanation would be incorporated into the survey's introductory spiel.

In terms of psychological or sociological incentives, surveyors may consider composing the introduction/selection sequence to point out the potential intangible benefits that participation may afford: for example, expressing one's own opinion; engaging in an interesting task (assuming the topic is likely to be interesting); and helping society (if there is a public policy link to the study). Other aspects of human nature that should be considered when composing fallback statements are altruism and compliance. Telling the potential respondent that he or she is helping the interviewer and the surveyor may be persuasive; wording a fallback statement to inform the respondent that the majority of persons contacted *do* participate (assuming this is an accurate statement for the survey organization) may help also. As a final consideration, having a fallback statement to help interviewers counter the attitudes of some respondents who say, "Let someone else do it," might also be considered.

CATI

A CATI system that controls the introductory sequence affords the opportunity to tailor the exact wording of the spiel to the individual respondent. To date, there is no literature on the effects that this individualized approach might have. In a panel survey, for example, in which information is known about respondents from their previous interviews, special introductions might be composed that incorporate, and thereby personalize, data about the respondent that was learned in an earlier wave (see Lavrakas, Settersten, & Maier, 1991). Even in a cross-sectional RDD CATI survey, information gathered in previous call-attempts that did not lead to an interview might be incorporated into the wording of the introduction used in subsequent call-attempts.

RESPONDENT SELECTION AND SCREENING TECHNIQUES

Even in the most poorly controlled telephone surveys there often is a selection of respondents from among the members of a sampling unit. (This section assumes that interviewers are not contacting persons whose names have been sampled from a list or are known otherwise.) Even an untrained interviewer will normally recognize that a potential respondent must be physically and intellectually able to answer the questionnaire. In some cases, though, common sense does not prevail and English-language interviews are attempted with persons who can barely understand English or those whose temporary or permanent mental capacity is diminished beyond the point of providing valid answers, thus adding to the survey's measurement error. It is not the purpose of this section to discuss ways to guard against these errors in judgment on the part of interviewers; this is addressed in Chapters 5 and 6. Rather, this section will review different respondent selection and screening procedures.

Although uncontrolled selection is never the recommended approach, it is instructive to begin by illustrating the problems that can be created by simply leaving it to interviewers to decide whom to interview within a sampling unit. The following section assumes that the telephone survey being conducted is an interview of individuals reporting on their *own* attitudes, behaviors, or experiences. If the purpose of a survey is to measure constructs that exist at the level of the sampling unit (e.g., number of working televisions in the household and whether any are connected to cable service), then any knowledgeable household informant could be interviewed without necessarily contributing either to noncoverage error or measurement error. In such cases, respondent selection from within a sampling unit is simply a matter of the interviewer reaching any eligible person as defined by the surveyor. (In this case, an easy and controlled approach is to have interviewers ask for the "woman of the household" if the telephone is answered by a woman, or for the "man of the household" if answered by a man.)

Uncontrolled Selection

In general population surveys in which there is no structured within-household respondent selection, interviewers simply try to interview anyone in the household who qualifies as an eligible. In many cases, age is the only criterion by which interviewers make the selection: for example, any person over the age of 17 years. In contrast, a survey may be a sampling of males' opinions and interviewers need only to speak with a male who is available in the household, if there is one. (Telephone surveys for market research dealing with traditional "masculine" products, e.g., chewing tobacco, often employ an uncontrolled within-unit selection of adult males.) Other surveys may have interviewers simply speak with a head of household, often allowing the household to define what this means. In each instance where a formal selection process is not printed on the introduction/selection sheet, interviewers merely ask to speak with any person fitting the eligibility requirement(s) immediately after they have read the introductory spiel.

Two types of problems can be created with uncontrolled respondent selection when a survey's purpose is to measure the levels at which variables exist within the target population. The first and more serious is that a representative sample from the population of interest is not likely to be interviewed due to likely within-sampling unit noncoverage error. If interviewers are allowed to choose whomever they wish who fits the eligibility requirements, the resulting sample will be disproportionately made up of those persons who are more likely to be available at the time interviewers call. In the general population, this commonly means women and older adults (see Salmon & Nichols, 1983). If several people are available who fit the eligibility requirements, then interviewers will naturally want to speak with the one who is available and/or is most willing to be interviewed. If this happens, then the resulting sample will be somewhat more likely to include younger and better educated persons. Unfortunately, the selection biases associated with availability and willingness cannot be expected to cancel each other out, thereby eliminating noncoverage error. Rather, the mix that will result will not be predictable from survey to survey, and cannot be defended as having high external validity.

A second problem with uncontrolled selection is one that may grow in time. As members of the public slowly become more sophisticated consumers of and participants in survey research, it is hoped that a survey of the general population that employs uncontrolled respondent selection will be regarded as unprofessional by more and more people. As it is in the best interest of both interviewers and the surveyor to impress upon potential respondents that they will not be wasting their time by participating in a sloppy survey (i.e., one with large total survey error and, therefore, likely to be invalid), compliance may be higher with a well-worded, nonintrusive, yet nevertheless formalized selection procedure.

Controlled Selection

During the past 30 years, most of the techniques that commonly have been employed for respondent selection are not ones that provide a true within-sampling unit probability sample. Instead, they were devised to provide a systematic means that does not allow an interviewer to select a respondent of her or his own choice. The techniques also were devised to be minimally intrusive while attempting to provide a demographically balanced sample of respondents across an entire survey. These nonprobability respondent selection techniques are discussed later in this section after first examining the standard probability selection procedure.

Kish Method of Random Selection

The most rigorous respondent selection method that is the accepted standard for in-person interviews was developed by Kish (1949, 1965). It can also be used in telephone surveys that require as complete a representation as possible of all eligibles from within sampling units.

It is important to note that even with use of the Kish method there is likely to be some small error in within-unit coverage. This occurs because not all sampling units (e.g., households) are willing or able to provide an enumeration of all eligibles. For example, Groves and Kahn (1979), in a reliability check of household composition, found that 9% of households gave discrepant information about the number of adults in the household, with the problem most likely associated with the presence of young adult members. In addition to error due to the purposeful misreporting of eligibles, not everyone will understand who is included in any given survey's definition of *eligible* as it is used in a selection sequence (see Maklan & Waksberg, 1988; Groves, 1989, pp. 108-115). This is more a problem in telephone surveys than in-person surveys, because the telephone interviewer is unable to resolve some problems that might otherwise be avoided with visual cues that would be present during an in-person interview (Massey, 1988).

Although considered a true probability selection technique in theory, the Kish method actually leads to an extremely small underrepresentation of the youngest of eligibles in households with a large number of eligibles (> 6). Nevertheless, the Kish method will minimize noncoverage within sampling units compared with other less rigorous selection methods (although, as noted below, it may increase nonresponse). As shown in Figure 4.3, immediately after the introductory spiel, the interviewer must identify all eligibles within the sampling unit. In most cases this means determining all who meet some age criterion living in a household. Some surveyors prefer to have interviewers identify eligibles by the relationships within the household, whereas others have interviewers ask for eligibles' first names. Either way, it is typical for interviewers to begin by identifying the household head(s) and then follow by listing other eligibles. For example, assuming the survey is sampling adults, an interviewer will most commonly begin by recording the husband and the wife since this is the most frequent adult composition in U.S. households.

Hello, my name is _____, and I'm calling from . . . * * * *insert introductory spiel* * *

May I please verify that is this _____? [VERIFY PHONE NUMBER]

In order to randomly pick one person in your household whom I can interview I need to begin by listing all persons in your household 18 years old or older. Could you just tell me their relationships to each other, not their names?

[AFTER LISTING PERSONS IN COLUMN 1 BELOW CONTINUE, UNLESS ONLY ONE ADULT, THEN DETERMINE AGE AND GO TO Q1:] Now I need to know the age of each person.

[AFTER LISTING AGES IN COLUMN 3 BELOW CONTINUE:] Now it will take me just a few seconds to use a selection chart I have here to determine the person I'm supposed to interview in your household.

LIST ALL PERSONS
AGE 18 AND OLDER IN DWELLING UNIT

NUMBER PERSONS 18 OR OVER IN THE FOLLOWING ORDER:

OLDEST MALE, NEXT OLDEST MALE, ETC.; FOLLOWED BY OLDEST FEMALE, NEXT OLDEST FEMALE, ETC. THEN USE SELECTION TABLE BELOW TO CHOOSE RESPONDENT.

RELATIONSHIP TO HEAD (1)	SEX (2)	AGE (3)	ADULT (4)	CHECK (5)
Husband M		52	2	
Wife F		50	4	✓
Daughter F		23	5	
Son M		19	3	
Husb. Father M		78	1	

SELECTION TABLE D

IF THE NUMBER OF ADULTS IN THE DWELLING IS:	INTERVIEW THE ADULT NUMBERED:
1	1
2	2
3	2
4	3
5	4
6 OR MORE	4

The selection chart indicates that in your household I'm supposed to interview _____ .
May I please speak with (her)(him)?

[IF DESIGNATED RESPONDENT IS SOMEONE OTHER THAN THE PERSON WITH WHOM YOU ARE SPEAKING, ASK TO SPEAK WITH THAT PERSON AND REPEAT INTRO BEFORE SKIPPING TO Q1]

[IF DESIGNATED RESPONDENT IS UNAVAILABLE, DETERMINE WHEN BEST TO CALL BACK AND LIST ON CALL-SHEET]

Figure 4.3. Example of Kish Selection Sheet.

After the interviewer has made certain that all eligibles are listed, the age of each of the eligibles is asked and recorded. The interviewer then pauses to check that the age of each person listed meets the age requirements of the survey, and then eliminates any who do not meet the requirements from further consideration. Then the interviewer rank-orders each eligible according to the following rule: oldest male numbered 1, next oldest male (if there is one) numbered 2, and so on through all males listed, then followed by oldest female, the next oldest female, and so forth. For example, consider a household composed of a husband, wife, their adult son, their adult daughter, and the husband's father (as shown in Figure 4.3). In this case, the father of the husband is assigned 1, the husband 2, the son 3, the wife 4, and the daughter 5. (If a surveyor preferred, the gender ordering could be reversed with females ordered before males; that is, the choice is an arbitrary one.)

Fortunately for those surveys that employ the Kish method, more than 90% of all U.S. households have less than four eligibles so that the time it commonly takes interviewers to list eligibles and their ages and to assign a selection number is relatively brief. In an in-person interview the household informant can see what the interviewer is doing. When the Kish method is used on the telephone it is prudent to have interviewers make a brief comment, as illustrated in Figure 4.3, to alert the listener as to why there is a slight pause at the time the ranking is performed.

After the numerical selection number is recorded for each eligible, the interviewer consults one of eight versions of a selection table that is printed on the introduction/selection sheet (see Figure 4.3). This selection table indicates which of the eligibles is the designated respondent associated with the particular call-sheet (i.e., sampling unit). In the selection table in Figure 4.3, an interviewer who had reached a household with five eligibles would interview the wife (#4).

Table 4.1 shows the selection information that should be printed in each of the eight versions of the selection table used with the Kish method. The first column in Table 4.1 also indicates the proportion in which each table is used within the survey. In manually pairing introduction/selection sheets with call-sheets the following order of selection tables would be used: A, A, B_1, B_2, C, C, D, D, E_1, E_2, F, F. In a CATI survey in which the introduction/selection sequence was controlled by the software, the eight versions would be randomly assigned to a household in their prescribed proportions.

As can be seen, the Kish method requires interviewers to request rather personal information of a household informant very early on after contact has been made. Good interviewers will be successful with Kish, despite

Table 4.1

Kish Selection Tables

Proportions of assigned tables	Table number	If the number of adults in household is:					
		1	2	3	4	5	6 or more
		Select adult numbered:					
1/6	A	1	1	1	1	1	1
1/12	B1	1	1	1	1	2	2
1/12	B2	1	1	1	2	2	2
1/6	C	1	1	2	2	3	3
1/6	D	1	2	2	3	4	4
1/12	E1	1	2	3	3	3	5
1/12	E2	1	2	3	4	5	5
1/6	F	1	2	3	4	5	6

SOURCE: Kish (1965).

its difficulty (see Czaja, Blair, & Sebestik, 1982). Less skilled interviewers, especially those without experience, are likely to have an especially high refusal rate (adding to nonresponse) and, furthermore, may not use the method properly (possibly adding to noncoverage error).

In sum, despite its advantage over other selection methods in minimizing the likelihood of within-unit noncoverage error when it is used properly, the Kish method may lead to increased levels of nonresponse and, thus, nonresponse error. As such, the surveyor is faced with the trade-off of deciding whether the potential benefits of the Kish method offset the potential disadvantages in terms of total survey error and total survey costs.

Birthday Methods for Respondent Selection

In the past decade, a different approach for yielding a random selection of respondents within sampling units has been explored (Oldendick, Sorenson, Tuchfarber, & Bishop, 1985; O'Rourke & Blair, 1983; Salmon & Nichols, 1983). These methods either ask for the eligible person within the sampling unit whose birthday was most recent or ask for the eligible who will have the next birthday. Due to their nonintrusive nature and the heterogeneous within-unit sample they produce, the birthday selection methods have been widely embraced by academic, public sector, and private sector surveyors. Theoretically, these methods could yield a true within-unit probability sample, but in practice this does not appear to occur (see Groves & Lyberg, 1988, p. 208).

Because the birthday selection methods are neither intrusive nor time-consuming, and are easy for interviewers to use, their appeal is great. After the introductory spiel, the interviewer asks for a respondent along the following lines, "For this survey, I'd like to speak with the person in your household, 18 years of age or older, who had the last [I.E., MOST RECENT] birthday." The interviewer must be able to explain that *last* means most recent, thus the capitalized reminder to the interviewer. Another advantage of the birthday methods in PAPI telephone surveys is that one introduction/selection sheet can be posted at each interviewing station rather than a separate copy being attached to every call-sheet, as is the case with the Kish method.

Because of the somewhat novel wording of this selection procedure, problems arise with household informants who do not immediately understand what the interviewer is getting at; thus, the importance of the interviewer being able to accurately convey the meaning of the "last birthday" (or "next birthday day") request. Furthermore, because the methods do not require any form of an enumeration of all eligibles with the sampling unit, the birthday methods cannot very well control for possible respondent self-selection (thus, possible bias) by informants who do not answer accurately.

There is evidence that suggests that the birthday methods lead to the correct eligible being interviewed in most, but not all, cases. Table 4.2 shows the proportion of months in which respondents reported they were born in two separate surveys NUSL conducted using the last birthday selection method, each with a sample size of over 1,000. The 1990 survey of the Chicago metropolitan area was conducted from late April through early June, whereas the 1992 survey of the United States was conducted from mid-March through the end of April. In each case, the greatest proportion of respondents reported birthdays occurring in months immediately prior to the field period, with a discernible trend (albeit an irregular one) for fewer persons to report birthdays in months more distant from the field period. This distribution of reported birthdays is what would be expected if the method were working properly.

In the 1992 survey, respondents were also asked to identify in what months all other eligibles (adults 18 years of age or older) in their households were born. Comparison of these data to the reported month of birth of the respondent suggests that in 20%-25% of the households there was another eligible whose birthday was more recent than that of the respondent (Lavrakas, Merkle, & Bauman, 1993). In other words, the "wrong" person, who apparently was a willing respondent, was interviewed. To the extent that this misselection of respondents commonly occurs with

Table 4.2

Reported Month of Birth for Respondents in Two RDD Surveys Using
the Last Birthday Selection Method

| | Percentage reporting each month | |
Month of birth	1990 Survey	1992 Survey
January	10.6	10.0
February	7.9	10.1
March	12.7	11.1
April	12.7	7.8
May	7.9	6.0
June	4.5	6.4
July	5.3	7.8
August	6.4	8.0
September	8.7	8.0
October	8.5	7.0
November	6.7	7.8
December	8.0	10.0

SOURCE: Northwestern University Survey Laboratory.
NOTE: The 1990 survey was conducted in the Chicago metropolitan area in late April and May of that year. The 1992 survey was conducted in the United States in late March and April of that year.

the birthday methods, it remains unclear what, if any, effects this has on within-unit coverage error. Surveyors would be wise to continue to follow the developing literature on the validity of the birthday methods, because despite their ease of use, their costs in terms of total survey error may outweigh their benefits.

Systematic Quota Selection Methods

The previous edition of this book presented a detailed explanation of three other systematic approaches to stratifying respondent selection within a sampling unit, such as a household, by gender and age (see Lavrakas, 1987, pp. 89-96). These methods can be used to provide within-household quota samples. However, since the mid-1980s they have been largely replaced by variants of the birthday methods. Due to this widespread shift in the practices of surveyors, this edition provides only a brief description of the quota selection methods.

Troldahl and Carter (1964) proposed a method less intrusive than the Kish approach for systematically (not randomly) selecting a respondent; however, compared with the birthday methods, it too is intrusive. Bryant (1975) suggested a modification of the Troldahl-Carter method to try to compensate for an undersampling of males. As described here, the

Trodalh-Carter-Bryant (T-C-B) selection method reflects a further refinement based on the findings of Czaja, Blair, and Sebestik (1982).

The T-C-B method requires the interviewer to ask two questions as part of the introduction/selection sequence: (a) "How many persons __ years or older live in your household, including yourself?"; and (b) "How many of these are women?" The age delimiter used in the first question is determined by the needs of each particular survey, but in most cases it is 18 (i.e., adults are selected).

Somewhat similar to the Kish approach, one of several versions of a selection matrix is then used by interviewers to objectively select the designated respondent based on the answers to the two questions. Also similar to Kish, a separate introduction/selection sheet must be attached (or paired in the case of CATI) to every call-sheet when the T-C-B method is employed. In theory, by mixing the versions of the selection matrices a survey will end with a proper balance (quota) of females and males and of younger and older adults compared with the target population. However, in practice even the prescribed combination of versions typically results in an undersampling of males, so it is recommended that the sampling pool controller take a daily count of males and females, compare it to the known ratio within the target population, and correct for discrepancies by selectively introducing either more or fewer new call-sheets with the selection matrix version(s) that will help correct the imbalance.

In the same way that Troldahl and Carter (1964) proposed a less intrusive respondent selection method than the Kish method, Hagen and Collier (1982) proposed a selection method even less intrusive than the T-C-B approach. Rather than following the introductory statement with a request for the number of persons over some age criterion, the Hagen-Collier approach simply asks outright for one of four types of respondents—youngest woman, oldest woman, youngest man, or oldest man—thereby avoiding the need to determine the number of possible eligibles in the household at the beginning of interviewer contact. Four versions of an introduction/selection sheet are used. If the sampling unit does not contain a person of the gender asked for, then interviewers need to be given proper follow-up instructions on the introduction/selection sheet. With the Hagen-Collier method, it is important that interviewers understand that in a household with only one woman, for example, she is both the youngest *and* the oldest woman. As with the T-C-B method, the four versions of the Hagen-Collier method need to be used in a ratio that yields a close approximation to the known distribution of males and females in the target population. In most cases if the four versions are used in equal proportion, there will be an undersampling of males, which will require increased usage of those

User Supplied Title

Phone Number
 ###-####
Hello, my name is _____, and I am a student at Northwestern University. My class is conducting a very short public opinion survey about heart transplant operations.

May I please verify that this is _____? **[VERIFY TELEPHONE NUMBER]**

For this survey, I need to speak with the YOUNGEST WOMAN in your household, if there is one.

[IF SPEAKING TO YOUNGEST WOMAN, SKIP TO Q1]

[IF SHE IS UNAVAILABLE, DETERMINE WHEN BEST TO CALL BACK]

[IF NO WOMAN IN HOUSEHOLD, ASK TO SPEAK TO YOUNGEST MAN—IF HE IS NOT AVAILABLE, ASK WHEN BEST TO CALL BACK]

[WHEN SELECTED RESPONDENT COMES TO PHONE, REPEAT INTRO IF NECESSARY, THEN SKIP TO Q1]

	Disposition	ID Number
Attempt 1:	_____	_____
Attempt 2:	_____	_____
Attempt 3:	_____	_____
Attempt 4:	_____	_____

Figure 4.4. Example of a Modified T-C-B With Call-Sheet.

introduction/selection sheets that ask for males as the survey progresses. Similar to T-C-B, the Hagen-Collier method also misses "middle-aged" persons in households with three or more eligibles of the same gender.

In some instances, even the Hagen-Collier method is overly complicated for use by inexperienced people who may be interviewing for only one or a few sessions, for example, as part of a short class project. In order to provide inexperienced interviewers with an easier selection method while simultaneously not relinquishing control of respondent selection entirely, I recommend employing two versions of an all-purpose, combined call-sheet and introduction/selection sheet. As shown in Figure 4.4, interviewers merely ask to speak with a male or a female in households with one such person (as with T-C-B) or ask to speak with the youngest male or female in households with more than one person of the same gender. There are two versions of this selection method: one that selects a female when there is at least one in the household and the other that selects a male. When this selection technique is used in surveys that last only a few days and thus can employ only a few callbacks, the effect of this oversampling of younger adult men and women often results in a preferred age mix, since these persons (especially younger adult males) are typically those hardest to reach in a short field period and otherwise will be undersampled. As with the full T-C-B method, a daily tally of males and females is recommended with this modified approach to determine the need to adjust the proportion of call-sheets that select for males.

None of these methods produces a within-household probability sample. They were developed for their convenience prior to the widespread use of the birthday methods. It may well be that their usefulness has passed.

Other Criteria for Respondent Selection

When a telephone survey requires only a certain type of respondent (e.g., women between the ages of 30 and 59 who are college graduates) then other respondent selection (or screening) methods will need to be employed. Some surveys will need to interview only heads of households or taxpayers. Others may need to select people who live within a relatively small geographic boundary. Still others will need to select some unique subsample of the general population.

Selecting for Head(s) of Household

The definition of who qualifies as a head of household has been a changing one in our society since the late 1960s. Traditionally, the head of household was defined as the husband when such a person existed, as was the case in about three of every four U.S. households as recent as the 1950s. Nowadays a more accepted and egalitarian definition defines *heads of household* as both the female and male in a primary couple in households with married or cohabiting adults. In single adult households, that adult is the head. If a survey needs to interview taxpayers (e.g., a mayor wants the opinions of his constituents before issuing a policy statement), then selecting for head of household generally will yield an appropriate within-household sample.

If a surveyor wants a fair balance of male and female heads of households, a selection method such as that shown in Figure 4.5 can be used. Somewhat similar to the Kish method, the interviewer begins by getting an enumeration of all adults based on their relationship to each other. In most cases it will then be obvious who is (are) the head(s). If there is any uncertainty, the interviewer must determine which person or couple is economically dominant, thus defining the head(s).

User Supplied Title

Hello, my name is _____, and I'm calling from . . .

May I please verify that is this _____? **[VERIFY TELEPHONE NUMBER]**

In order to systematically select which adult to interview in your household, would you please tell me how many adults 18 years old or older live there?

_____ Number of Adults 18 Years or Older

[IF "ONE", ASK FOR THAT ADULT, REPEAT INTRO IF NECESSARY, AND SKIP TO Q1]

I don't need any names but would you also tell me their relationship to each other?

[ENUMERATE ADULT MEMBERS OF HOUSEHOLD (E.G., "HUSBAND," "WIFE," "HUSBAND'S FATHER," ETC.)]:

(1) _____

(2) _____

(3) _____   ** INTERVIEW HUSBAND/

(4) _____   MALE IN PRIMARY COUPLE **

(5) _____

(6) _____

[IF PRIMARY COUPLE NOT CLEAR, PICK ECONOMIC DOMINANT BY ASKING]:

Who provides the major share of financial support for the family?

[CHECK RESPONDENT, THEN CONTINUE]:

For this survey I need to interview _____. May I please speak with (him)(her)?

[IF DESIGNATED RESPONDENT IS UNAVAILABLE, DETERMINE WHEN BEST TO CALL BACK AND LIST ON CALL-SHEET]

Figure 4.5. Example of Head of Household Selection.

Two versions of this selection method are printed and paired with call-sheets. One version, as shown in Figure 4.5, asks for the male head in households with a primary couple, whereas the other version asks for the female head. When NUSL has employed this selection technique in PAPI surveys, these versions have been printed on pink and blue stock, further reinforcing for interviewers which head will be the designated respondent in a household with a primary couple. In households with only one head, then that person is designated as the respondent regardless of the color stock on which the form is printed.

When a survey selects for head of household, it is not unusual to sample females 60% or more of the time, especially in urban areas where women are the heads of many single-parent households. Demographic patterns within the sampling area should be known a priori so that the sampling pool controller can adjust the use of the different versions of the introduction/selection sheets if daily tallies of males and females indicate an imbalance in the expected (or preferred) gender ratio.

Screening for Likely Voters

Many surveys deal with political issues and in some the surveyor may want to interview only "likely voters." In these cases the surveyor must construct a screening sequence to identify an eligible respondent. Although there is considerable anecdotal information about how political pollsters identify likely voters, there is no definitive literature on the subject (see Lewis, 1991). My own approach is similar to that which many other surveyors appear to employ: to begin the selection/screening sequence that follows the introductory spiel with a question to verify that the potential respondent lives within the municipal boundaries of the forthcoming election. Then the individual is asked if he or she is currently registered to vote in the municipality. The potential respondent is then asked about having voted in the last election (assuming he or she was old enough at the time) and then is asked to indicate the likelihood of voting in the forthcoming election. If at anytime during this screening sequence the individual responds negatively (e.g., "I didn't have time to vote in the last election" or "I'm unlikely to vote in the next election"), then contact with that individual is politely terminated (i.e., no interview is conducted). At this point, the surveyor may choose to have interviewers attempt to identify another possible eligible within the sampling unit or may choose to have the interviewer proceed to a new call-sheet.

Geographic Screening

Sometimes a telephone survey will reach households that are outside the boundaries of the sampling area because telephone prefix boundaries do not always conform to those of the sampling area. In the case where the boundaries of the sampling area coincide with municipal boundaries, geographic screening is straightforward: Immediately after the introductory spiel, the interviewer merely asks, "Do you live in _____?" where the blank contains the name of some recognized geopolitical area (e.g., Cook County, Boston, Wayne County, San Jose, Dade County, etc.).

If the person being spoken to indicates that the household is not located in the specified area the interviewer politely explains why an interview cannot be conducted before terminating contact. If the household inform- ant is uncertain whether the household is located within the sampling area the interviewer should ask to speak with some other knowledgeable person in the household.

In all cases in which a household is excluded because the interviewer is told it is located outside the specified area, a special disposition code is needed for the call-sheet. The sampling pool controller can then review call-sheets with this disposition, noting if there are more of these ineligi- bles than had been anticipated. If there is any uncertainty about the accuracy of household informants in responding to the geographic screener then some proportion of these dispositions should be checked via a reverse directory in order to make an informed decision about whether or not to call these numbers again.

Sampling boundaries that conform to neither prefix boundaries nor municipal boundaries are much more troublesome and often rule against RDD because of a likely increase in both nonresponse error and coverage error. Nonresponse is likely to increase in any survey that requires a potential respondent to answer detailed questions about her or his place of residence soon after contact has been made (see Lavrakas, 1987, pp. 71-74). This may be due to a perceived invasion of privacy and/or to the embarrassment or annoyance of being "tested" on geographic information (e.g., "Do you live east or west of South 47th Street?") about which the individual is uncertain. In terms of increases in coverage errors, geographic screening is likely to lead to both errors of omission and errors of commission; the former occurring when people who live inside the target area answer in ways that screen themselves out (false negatives) and the latter occurring when people who live outside the target area answer in ways that screen themselves in (false positives).

When faced with these challenges a surveyor should pretest the geo- graphic screener to assess its validity. Consideration should be given also to generating the sampling pool from a reverse directory, if one exists for the sampling area; although the advantage gained from targeting calls into exact geographic boundaries may be offset by the different type of noncover- age that will generally result from using only listed telephone numbers.

Selecting/Screening for Other Factors

Within reason, telephone survey respondents can be selected along several attributes. Through careful development and pretesting, a surveyor should be able to devise a workable selection sequence without appreciably increasing noncoverage or nonresponse.

In those instances in which selection criteria are complicated, it may be wise to intersperse them in the early sequencing of questions with an understanding that the interview will be terminated if it is determined that the respondent is not truly eligible. In other words, it may be necessary to bear the cost of starting the interview with persons who may not be eligible, rather than loading all selection criteria at the point of contact, thereby producing too many refusals by asking too many personal questions before establishing adequate interviewer-respondent rapport.

For example, Figure 4.6 shows a selection sequence that was developed by NUSL to screen for any male in a household over 24 years of age, whose racial/ethnic background was black or white, and who was not of Arab or Jewish descent. The sequence of questions required the interviewer to first ask to speak with a male, 25 years of age or older, if there was one. In households without such a person, contact was politely terminated. Once the interviewer reached a male of appropriate age, the additional demographic screening questions for race, ethnicity, and religion were asked. If at any point in this sequence it was determined that the person was ineligible, contact was politely terminated.

This selection/screening sequence is preferred to one which would follow the introductory spiel by stating, "For this survey, I need to speak with any male in your household, over the age of 24, who is black or white, but not an Arab or a Jew, if there is such a person." Not only would a sequence such as this be misunderstood frequently, interviewers would still have to go through the three screener questions to make absolutely certain they were speaking to an eligible.

Even more complicated selection criteria can be used effectively in telephone surveys. Through the use of a pretest the surveyor should be able to refine the wording so as to avoid increasing total survey error. Ultimately it is the ability of the interviewers who use the required selection procedure that will play a large part in determining how many potential respondents are lost due to refusals shortly after contact or to misunderstood selection criteria.

ADVANCE CONTACT OF RESPONDENTS

As part of the endeavor to select respondents and secure their cooperation telephone surveys sometimes afford the opportunity for the surveyor

Hello, my name is _____, and I'm calling from the Northwestern University Survey Lab (in Evanston). We are conducting a public opinion survey about international affairs and the Middle East.

May I please verify that this is _____? **[VERIFY TELEPHONE NUMBER]**

For this survey, I need to speak with *a man, 25 years of age or older*. Does anyone in your household fit into this category?

[IF TOLD NO MAN LIVES IN HOUSEHOLD, POLITELY TERMINATE]

[IF MAN IN HOUSEHOLD IS NOT 25 YEARS OR OLDER, POLITELY TERMINATE]

[IF ELIGIBLE MALE IS NOT HOME, DETERMINE WHEN TO CALL BACK]

[CONTINUE WHEN SPEAKING TO ELIGIBLE MALE, REPEAT INTRO IF NECESSARY:]

In addition to questions about international affairs and the Middle East, throughout the survey I will also be asking you some questions about yourself. Now I'll begin by asking you three short background questions.

S1. What is your racial background? Are you . . .

Asian,	1 **[POLITELY TERMINATE]**
Black,	2
Hispanic, or	3 **[POLITELY TERMINATE]**
White?	4
Other	5 **[POLITELY TERMINATE]**
Refused	8 **[POLITELY TERMINATE]**

S2. Are you of Arabic or Jewish decent?

Yes	1 **[POLITELY TERMINATE]**
No	2
Refused	8 **[POLITELY TERMINATE]**

S3. What is your religious preference? Are you . . .

Catholic,	1
Protestant,	2
Jewish, or	3 **[POLITELY TERMINATE]**
Something else? (specify _____)	4
Refused	8 **[POLITELY TERMINATE]**

Figure 4.6. Example of Screener-Selection Sheet.

to consider deploying some form of advance contact of the sampling unit (see Dillman et al., 1976; Frey, 1989, pp. 127-130). The basic rationale underlying this additional effort (and cost) is that a potential respondent will be more readily persuaded to participate if he or she has been "warmed up" by advance notification of the survey than if he or she merely receives a "cold call" from an interviewer without any advance warning. Traugott et al. (1987) reported experimental evidence that advance contact increased their telephone survey response rates by more than 10 percentage points. The ultimate goal of committing the additional resources needed for advance contacts is to lessen the chance for nonresponse error and, in some cases, coverage error, thereby lowering the likelihood that these factors will contribute to total survey error.

If a telephone survey employs a sampling frame that contains street addresses, mailing an advance letter to the sampling unit or respondent is as simple as stuffing the envelopes and sending them out, once the letters have been prepared and signed. Even if RDD is used all is not lost provided there are sufficient resources, since it is possible that a commercial street address list or data base (or reverse directory) can be purchased, and addresses can then be matched with the majority, but not all, of the telephone numbers in the sampling pool in most sampling areas.

Experience at NUSL suggests that advance contact is especially valuable in surveys of elite target populations, such as busy CEOs, lawyers, physicians, and so forth. In this case, a two-step process can be followed whereby a preliminary telephone call is made to the respondent's office to learn her or his fax number; advance contact is then made via a faxed letter. Several telephone surveys of elite populations conducted by NUSL in the past five years, in which some form of advance contact was used, have led to response rates in the 60%-80% range. (Of note, in all of these surveys allowance was made for extensive callbacks and the scheduling of interviews at the respondents' convenience.)

Regarding the form and content of the advance letter, it should be on letterhead, which serves to legitimize the survey endeavor, and the letter should be no longer than one page (see Frey, 1989, p. 129). A brief explanation of the survey's purpose, content, length, and sponsorship should be included. Confidentiality should also be mentioned, as should the willingness of interviewers to call back at a time convenient to the respondent. The surveyor also should look for ways to personalize the advance contact, such as, personally signing all the letters in nonblack ink, and having the envelopes posted with stamps rather than a postage meter (assuming the mail is used, not a fax). A final point to remember is to incorporate an explicit reference about the advance contact into the introductory spiel and fallback statements that interviewers will use.

In some telephone surveys, advance contact can do more that merely alert the respondent to a forthcoming attempt to conduct an interview. For example, instructions and/or visual aids may need to be provided for a complicated survey, or the respondent may need to assemble information from personal files prior to the interview.

Advance contact takes time and adds costs. As such it remains the surveyor's responsibility to make an a priori decision about the value of allocating resources to this end.

EXERCISES

Exercise 4.1:   Write an introductory spiel for an RDD survey designed to sample adults' satisfaction with local government services within a local municipality (county, city, or town). Assume that the survey is commissioned by the local municipality's governing body (e.g., county board, mayor's office, or town council).

Exercise 4.2:   Using the introductory spiel written in Exercise 4.1, develop an introduction/selection sheet that utilizes any of the controlled selection methods reviewed in this chapter to select one adult per sampled household.

Exercise 4.3:   Continuing from the two previous exercises, write the text of a fallback statement for use by interviewers if they were asked by potential respondents how their confidentiality will be protected if they participate in this survey commissioned by the local government. Direct the fallback statement especially to those who are apprehensive that their names may be given to the local governing body. Limit the fallback statement to 100 words or less.

Exercise 4.4:   Write the text of an advance letter that could be sent to each of the potential respondents for whom addresses could be secured in the above survey.

Exercise 4.5:   Contact a local marketing research firm and determine the respondent selection method(s) typically employed with general population surveys, and why the firm prefers this (these) method(s). Explain your findings in a written narrative, including any critique you feel necessary of the firm's choice(s).

Exercise 4.6:   For a national RDD survey measuring shopping habits, write and lay out an introduction and a respondent selection sequence that will screen for the following type of eligible: a man, 25-44 years of age, who also has at least some graduate school experience.

Exercise 4.7:   Modify the selection sequence developed in Exercise 4.6 so that it also screens out all persons who do not have an American Express card, Master-Card, or Visa card.

5

Supervision I: Structuring Interviewers' Work

As Groves (1989) notes, "interviewers are the medium through which measurements are taken in [personal and telephone] surveys" (p. 404). This includes not only asking questions and recording responses, but also processing the sample and securing respondent cooperation. Given the central role of interviewers it is not surprising that they can add significant bias and variance to survey measures. However, there are many strategies for reducing interviewer-related error (see Fowler & Mangione, 1990, p. 9) that too often go unused.

Interviewing is a part of the telephone surveying process that is much more a craft than a science. This chapter discusses the importance of the interviewer in telephone surveys. The purpose is to inform the reader about the ways in which a surveyor can structure various stages of the survey process, ranging from interviewer recruitment to on-the-job-training, to obtain interviewers who will produce high-quality data by contributing little, if anything, to measurement error, nonresponse error, or noncoverage error.

The chapter begins with a brief discussion of the issue of control of interviewing quality in telephone surveys versus personal interviewing. Next, considerations are reviewed about the ways in which paid and unpaid (volunteer) telephone interviewers can be recruited. Included is advice on how to screen potential interviewers before making a final decision to use them for a survey.

The paramount importance of interviewer training prior to the start of each survey is reviewed, regardless of whether the survey will be with PAPI or CATI. A detailed explanation is provided about the two basic parts of presurvey training: general and survey-specific. This includes explicit training in the proper use of the questionnaire's closed- and open-end items, along with nonbiased probing of ambiguous or incomplete responses. Training to reduce nonresponse is also reviewed. Next, the never-ending aspect of on-the-job training is discussed. The chapter concludes with a brief review of the issues regarding the interviewer's effect on total survey error and of the approaches the surveyor might employ to assess the size of these potential effects.

QUALITY CONTROL IN TELEPHONE
VERSUS PERSONAL INTERVIEWING

This book has emphasized that the potentially large advantage that telephone surveys have over other modes of gathering survey data is the opportunity for control provided by a centralized data collection process. If this control is properly exercised, the resulting data should be of high quality from the standpoint of lessening possible error due to interviewers' behaviors.

Surprisingly, although many surveyors appear to recognize the importance of a representative sampling pool, a low rate of nonresponse, and a well-constructed questionnaire, often they are lax in the control they institute over the telephone interviewing process. It is as though they assume that once one has a good questionnaire and a valid sampling procedure, successful data collection will naturally follow. The reality of gathering survey data via telephone within the perspective of total survey error, however, shows the folly of this assumption: Unless data are gathered in a controlled and standardized fashion, they will not be comparable across respondents, thereby invalidating the survey (see Fowler & Mangione, 1990) and wasting whatever resources have been committed.

Cost appears to be the primary reason for the lack of adequate attention given to rigorous control of interviewing in telephone surveys. Although it is expensive to institute strict and constant controls of telephone interviewers, in the absence of such a system one should be concerned that money spent on other parts of the survey enterprise (e.g., sampling) may be money wasted.

Another reason may be that many surveyors traditionally learned about survey methods via books about and experience with face-to-face interviewing. With personal interviewing, the role of interviewers and supervisors in collecting data differs from that in telephone interviewing in significant operational ways. For example, with face-to-face interviewing, it is neither feasible nor practical to immediately check completed questionnaires and provide immediate feedback to interviewers. Furthermore, unlike telephone surveys, personal interviewing does not allow for the supervisor to monitor the progress of any ongoing interview.

Because of these and other factors the interviewer plays a more active role in creating the data in personal interviewing than needs to be accepted in telephone interviewing. No matter how superior a group of interviewers may be, the level of standardization that practically can be achieved with face-to-face interviews is not likely to approach what can and should be expected with quality centralized telephone interviewing.

RECRUITMENT AND HIRING OF INTERVIEWERS

General Considerations

A basic consideration regarding interviewers is whether they are paid for their work or unpaid, such as volunteers or students who must do interviewing as part of course work. When a telephone survey employs paid interviewers there should be a greater likelihood of higher quality interviewing due to several factors. In situations in which interviewers are paid, there can be a careful selection of the most skilled individuals. With unpaid interviewers there is much less control over who will not be allowed to interview. Paid interviewers are more likely to have an objective detachment from the survey's purpose. In contrast, unpaid interviewers often have expectancies of the data; that is, volunteers by nature are often committed to an organization's purpose in conducting a survey and may hold preconceived notions of results, thereby altering their behavior as interviewers and contributing bias (measurement error) to the data they gather. Similarly, students who interview for academic credit often have an interest in the survey's outcome, especially if it is their class's own project.

Regardless of whether interviewers are paid or unpaid, it is recommended that each interviewer enter into a written agreement with the surveyor. This should include a clause about not violating respondents' confidentiality. Although the written agreement may be standard practice for those who employ paid interviewers, it rarely is employed by those who utilize unpaid interviewers. Yet the National Organization for Voluntary Action (NOVA) strongly recommends that volunteers be treated like paid employees when it comes to holding them accountable for what they have volunteered to do. NOVA believes that having volunteers sign a nonbinding work contract can be very effective in reinforcing the importance of the work the volunteer has agreed to do. Unpaid telephone interviewers need to know their time is not being wasted, and a written contract can be a symbolic affirmation of the importance of the work.

Interviewers' training should be consistent regardless of whether they are paid or unpaid, but recruitment takes a somewhat different tack depending upon the type of interviewer being sought. Nonetheless, there are some constants that should be included in the recruitment of all interviewers. First, it must be made very clear to all interviewers that telephone surveys normally require "standardized survey interviewing" (see Fowler & Mangione, 1990)—a highly structured and rather sterile style of interviewing. Standardized survey interviewing does not allow for creativity on the part of interviewers in the ordering or wording of particular questionnaire items or in deciding who can be interviewed. Furthermore, all prospective telephone interviewers should be informed about the constant monitoring done by supervisors, including listening to ongoing interviews.

Informing prospective interviewers of features such as these in advance of making a final decision about their beginning to work will create realistic expectations. In the case of paid interviewers, it may discourage those who are not likely to conform to highly structured situations from applying. Additional considerations for each type of interviewer follow.

Paid Interviewers

With paid interviewers the surveyor has the opportunity of enlisting the most qualified individuals: *those most likely to follow the procedures which are instituted to minimize total survey error.* Thus the recruitment and hiring process should be structured with this goal in mind. This can be achieved best by using a careful screening procedure and by offering a good wage to attract persons with greater ability and experience who might otherwise not be as interested in telephone interviewing. Simply stated, the more one pays interviewers, the more one can (and should) expect from them, both in terms of quality and quantity. It is even possible that a preferred cost/benefit ratio (in terms of reduced total survey error) will be achieved by employing relatively fewer expensive, yet skilled, interviewers whose quality and productivity are high than with more inexpensive, yet less skilled, interviewers.

In hiring new interviewers advertisements should mention the starting hourly wage and the part-time nature of the work. For example, interviewers at NUSL typically work 12 to 20 hours per week. At larger facilities, such as the Survey Research Center at the University of Michigan, interviewers work longer stints (18 to 35 hours per week) due in part to the larger and more constant volume of survey work in which larger facilities engage (Groves, 1989).

It is recommended also that the phrase, "experience preferred," be included in the ad because it helps to screen out some marginal applicants. In this case, it is experience with telephone surveying, not telemarketing, that is preferred (see Frey, 1989, p. 220). (In fact, some individuals with only telemarketing experience appear to have considerable difficulty in adapting to the very different behaviors that are required for standardized telephone survey interviewing.) If interviewers are being hired for CATI surveys, experience with typing and computers is also preferred. The ads used by the NUSL list a starting hourly wage that is approximately twice the current minimum wage; the latter figure was $4.25 per hour at the time this edition text was written. The willingness to pay new interviewers this well reflects primarily the quality of individual NUSL wants to employ and retain and, secondarily, reflects the local cost of living in the Chicago metropolitan area.

I also recommend that the ad should list a telephone number to call, not an address to visit in person. The explicit purpose in screening a potential telephone interviewer via the telephone is to assess her or his "telephone presence." Were prospective interviewers to apply in person, nonverbal behavior might be confounded with any assessment made by hiring personnel. In the current era, prior to the possible widespread future use of the videophone in telephone surveying, it is an applicant's voice and other verbal behavior, not his or her appearance, that will affect success as a telephone interviewer. As such, there is little reason to see the applicant at the preliminary stages of hiring. (This is not meant to suggest that no important information can be gleaned in person. For example, a prospective interviewer could be tested for reading skills as part of in-person screening.) In screening applicants via telephone an interviewer screening form should be used that includes "first impression" ratings about the applicant's verbal demeanor along with demographic and background information. The more experienced the personnel who screen applicants, the more valid should be the ratings.

Survey administrators may be concerned with whether there are any demographic characteristics that are associated with high quality interviewing—such as gender, age, or education—and whether hiring decisions should take these characteristics into account. Within the perspective of wanting to avoid hiring practices that might be discriminatory, it should be noted that, "other than good reading and writing skills and a reasonably pleasant personality, [there appear to be] no other credible selection criteria for distinguishing among potential interviewers" (Fowler & Mangione, 1990, p. 140). Even in the case of strong regional accents, Bass and Tortora (1988) reported no interviewer-related effects.

On the other hand, if the survey topic is related to interviewer demographics, there is consistent evidence that unwanted interviewer/respondent effects occur which increase total survey error (see Fowler & Mangione, 1990, pp. 98-105). For example, a survey on sexual harassment conducted while this edition was being written found that male respondents were twice as likely to report having sexually harassed someone at work if they were interviewed by a male versus a female interviewer (Lavrakas, 1992). In such cases, hiring criteria certainly must take into account the needs of the survey and consider interviewer demographics in a nondiscriminatory manner. In sum, if there is a clear and credible reason to use demographic selection criteria which is related to reduced interviewer-related effects, then one is not discriminating against those who do not "qualify" demographically.

Given the part-time nature of most telephone interviewing employment, the manner in which hiring and training are organized should result in a self-selection process that leads applicants who are not likely to be good interviewers to decide for themselves to withdraw their applications. Based upon the preliminary screening interview, applicants who are judged to have adequate potential are chosen for training. The self-selection process continues to work at this point. For example, if during the application interview it is made clear that reliability of attendance is a very important employment criterion (i.e., reporting on time to every interviewing session for which one is scheduled), prompt attendance to the training session(s) is another way to judge the suitability of a particular applicant. After this, on-the-job performance should be used to decide whom to continue to employ as an interviewer (see Chapter 6).

Unpaid Interviewers

There is far less control over persons who are available to serve as interviewers when a survey cannot or does not pay for their time. In situations in which students do interviewing as part of a class project, normally all class members must participate in the data collection. In this case the surveyor/instructor has to make do with whoever is enrolled, although with adequate training and intensive on-the-job supervision most students will do acceptable interviewing. With volunteer interviewers, self-selection and screening criteria similar to those discussed above for paid interviewers can be employed. But in the end, a surveyor must be willing to inform a volunteer that he or she appears better suited for some other type of service and should not interview.

TRAINING SESSIONS

Fowler and Mangione (1986) conducted a comprehensive study of how training is related to interviewer-related effects in survey data. The effects uncovered by the study were relatively small in magnitude, but consistent enough to lead the researchers to conclude that "interviewers need supervised practice in general interviewing skills . . . [training] that used only reading, lectures, and a demonstration interview was insufficient" (Fowler & Mangione, 1990, pp. 117-118). These results provide support for the importance of multifaceted interviewer training.

A central part of interviewer training is the formal training sessions that are held before each new survey commences. The purpose of this form of training is to provide interviewers (and supervisors) with enough background information and experience with survey procedures and materials that they are well-prepared to begin on-the-job training and/or actual interviewing. The information that should be conveyed to interviewers in training sessions is of two types: (a) general information about standard work practices and expectations; and (b) specific information about the particular survey.

Training sessions always should be conducted by skilled personnel, preferably the survey's field director. This person should be experienced with all aspects of the survey process, ideally having been both a telephone interviewer and a supervisor. The trainer must be articulate and organized: able to communicate with interviewers in a structured fashion while remaining sufficiently flexible to deal with unanticipated issues that may arise during the training session. Ultimately, it is the trainer's responsibility to instill the importance of quality interviewing upon those being trained and to make them ready for the next step, be it additional training or the start of actual interviewing.

To facilitate training sessions, each survey organization should develop an instructional manual for interviewers (and supervisors) that contains an explanation and elaboration of the procedures the organization considers to be essential for standardized survey interviewing. The manual should cover the issues that are discussed in the training sessions (see below). The interested reader is referred to Frey's (1989, pp. 222-233) discussion of telephone interviewer training manuals.

Training for General Work Expectancies

The following issues should be addressed in the part of training that covers general practices and expectancies:

1. what makes a good telephone interviewer, including behaviors related to processing the sampling pool, introducing the survey, selecting and securing the cooperation of the correct respondent, and administering the questionnaire in a standardized fashion;

2. how interviewing is monitored, including an explication of standards for quality and quantity; and

3. the particulars of employment with the organization or person conducting the survey.

Fowler and Mangione (1990) suggest that prospective interviewers cannot be expected to behave acceptably as standardized survey interviewers with less than 20-30 hours of training. This should be considered by those planning for interviewer training and the cost associated with it.

Quality Telephone Interviewing

Every training session should include a detailed discussion (or review) of the behavioral characteristics that are exhibited by a good interviewer, even if only for review. The reader may disagree with some of the specific suggestions that follow, but it can be agreed that interviewers need to know what verbal behavior is expected of them.

Regardless of whether PAPI or CATI is used, a good telephone interviewer properly uses the survey's call-sheet, introduction and selection procedure, fallback statements, and questionnaire in an energetic fashion, but does not sacrifice quality for mere quantity. Therefore, interviewers must be trained to realize that there is considerably more to quality telephone interviewing than merely reading questions in a standardized fashion and recording answers.

The particulars concerning a survey's specific disposition codes, introduction, selection procedure, fallback statements, and questionnaire should be saved for the second part of the training. In the first part interviewers should learn about the generic aspects of all the steps that make up the total interviewing process and the relationship of these aspects to minimizing total survey error (see Fowler & Mangione, 1990). In fact, structuring the general instruction around the concept of total survey error (without making it overly academic) is highly recommended.

Instruction should be provided about speaking in a pleasant manner, without also biasing (i.e., reinforcing) certain types of responses. Interviewers should be warned against becoming an "on-the-phone therapist" when respondents want to go beyond the specifics of the questionnaire to discuss their own opinions or problems in detail. Interviewers must understand that they constantly must strive to retain control of the pacing and flow of the survey process. (Ideally, the questionnaire will be both worded and formatted in a way that helps the interviewer retain this control.)

In many survey situations, interviewers should behave somewhat like an intelligent automaton. They should not let their own personalities bias answers by being either too enthusiastic or too detached. A balance must be struck between these extremes, so that respondents can give their own answers uninfluenced by any expectations they may perceive on the part of interviewers (see Fowler & Mangione, 1990, pp. 48-50).

Fowler and Mangione (1990) define standardized survey interviewing as occurring when "interviewers ask questions only as worded, give only limited explanations about what is expected beyond the initial question, and write down answers verbatim" (p. 68). They explain that this includes "[probing] for clarification and elaboration in a nondirective way" and "[communicating] a neutral, nonjudgmental stance with respect to the substance of the answers" (p. 33).

At the same time respondents must know they are being interviewed by another person, not by an impersonal recording machine (as is the case in some telephone "surveys" conducted by some telemarketers). An interviewer must be allowed, and should be expected, to exercise some personal discretion on how to handle different types of respondents without making comments that are likely to bias responses.

The trainer should also consider the value of having interviewers understand the task facing survey respondents. Groves's (1989, pp. 407-440) review of the cognitive science literature relevant to this process can be especially useful to anyone planning to incorporate this type of information into the general training an interviewer receives. For example, it may be beneficial for interviewers to recognize the five stages in which respondents must engage to be able to answer a survey item: (a) previous encoding of information relevant to the item being asked; (b) comprehension of the meaning of the survey item; (c) retrieval in memory of relevant knowledge; (d) judgment of an appropriate answer among alternative answers; and (e) communication of the answer to the interviewer.

Nondirective Probing and Feedback

In the first part of training, the trainer should explain how interviewers are expected to engage in nondirective probing of respondents who have answered in some irrelevant or ambiguous fashion without biasing the responses. Interviewers should also understand how to give other feedback to respondents in a nondirective manner. Charles Cannell, a leading researcher in survey interviewer behavior and interviewer-related effects, suggests that the exchange that interviewers have with respondents in probing (following up) preliminary answers or giving other feedback should focus on the behavior (activity) the respondent is engaged in—answering questions—and not on the affect communicated in those answers (Cannell, 1991). For example, nonbiasing comments by an interviewer that focus on activity, not affect, would include, "This is useful information," or "This is the kind of information we need to get," and "Could you be more specific on that last point?" Interviewers should be trained to understand why these types of communications are preferred to ones that focus more on affect, such as, "That's too bad that happened but it's important that you've mentioned it." Fowler and Mangione (1990, pp. 37-46) and Frey (1989, pp. 224-225) provide detailed discussion and examples of the use of nonbiasing probes and feedback.

The manner in which a questionnaire is constructed, regardless of PAPI or CATI, also can help interviewers with probing and feedback through the use of specific examples of nondirective probes and neutral feedback comments, which can be written into the questionnaire. Interviewers need to be trained to exercise proper discretion in using these printed comments, which are thought to reduce interviewer-related variance. In addition, the manner in which terms are defined, or not defined, within the questionnaire will influence how well interviewers respond to respondents' requests for an explanation of what something means. In the absence of an explicit definition written into the questionnaire, interviewers should be trained to usually respond, "Whatever it means to you."

Refusal Avoidance Training

The single factor that seems to differentiate the best of interviewers from those who are not so good is the ability to handle difficult respondents and outright refusals. The part of the training session that covers general expectations therefore should include a detailed discussion of the nature of refusals and explicit advice on how to be politely persuasive without being overly aggressive. The interested reader is encouraged to study Groves's review of the social science literature on persuasion and compliance as it relates to respondents' willingness to participate in surveys and interviewing strategies to reduce nonresponse (see Groves, 1989, pp. 215-236).

Consistent with what I wrote in the original edition of this book, I continue to believe that it is best to assume that all potential respondents need to be provided incentives for participating. With most respondents it seems to be enough incentive if they are told they are being helpful by providing answers; for others, it appears to make them feel important to know that it is *their* opinions that are being sought.

But for 20%-30% of all potential respondents in surveys both of the general public and of special populations, interviewers will have to work harder at "selling" the interview. In these difficult cases one option is to assume that the timing of the contact is wrong and to call back on another occasion. Interviewers might be trained to make a statement such as, "I'm sorry we've bothered you at what apparently is a bad time for you." Interviewers must then exercise discretion on a case-by-case basis either by asking if there is a better time to call back, by stating simply that a callback will be made, or by not saying anything else. Another option is to "plead" with the potential respondent. When a telephone questionnaire is a relatively short one (i.e., 10 minutes or less), an interviewer can try to convince a reluctant respondent that it will not take very long. Another tactic to counter reluctance is to state that any question that the respondent is uncomfortable answering may be left unanswered. (Although this could increase item nonresponse, experience suggests that it is more likely to put respondents at ease without actually contributing to more missing data.) Also, interviewers can be trained to give several levels of assurance of both the legitimacy and importance of the survey through use of the survey's fallback statements. Here it is useful for interviewers to be able to provide the sponsor's name and telephone number in case the respondent wants further verification. However, simply providing such assurances often goes a long way toward alleviating the concerns of reluctant respondents.

A last resort for interviewers to consider is to remind the respondent that by cooperating, the respondent is helping the interviewer earn a living (or for the unpaid interviewer, cooperation is helping the interviewer fulfill her or his obligation). By personalizing the issue of cooperation, the interviewer neither is referring to an abstract incentive, such as "to help plan better social programs," nor is appealing in the name of a third party (the survey's sponsor). Rather the reluctant respondent may be persuaded to feel the satisfaction of knowing that he or she is directly helping the person who is doing the interviewing. (As is discussed later in this chapter, the mode of payment used with interviewers may affect the resourcefulness with which interviewers pursue potential refusals.)

In addition to training interviewers about what to say to minimize the refusals they experience, there should be training about how to say it in terms of both attitude and voice. Collins et al. (1988) reported findings that less successful interviewers, when confronted with problems, "showed a lack of confidence and a tendency to panic; they seemed unprepared for problems, gave in too easily, and failed to avoid 'deadends' " (p. 229). The confidence that successful interviewers feel is conveyed in the way they speak. Oksenberg and Cannell (1988) reported that "dominance" appears to win out, with interviewers with low refusal rates being "generally more potent" (p. 268), rather than trying to be overly friendly, ingratiating, and/or nonthreatening. In terms of interviewers' voices, the Oksenberg and Cannell research found that those who spoke faster, louder, with greater confidence, and in a "falling" tone (declarative vs. interrogative) had the lowest refusal rates.

In a time of increasing nonresponse rates, and with refusals making up the largest proportion of nonresponse in telephone surveys, interviewers must be provided with explicit refusal avoidance training. As such, it is the responsibility of surveyors and trainers to keep abreast of the developing literature in this very important field of survey methodology.

As noted in Chapter 3, refusal conversion is becoming a standard part of many quality survey endeavors. Training for refusal conversions should not be done as part of the general training that all interviewers receive. Rather, it should be provided to those interviewers who will participate in conversion attempts and at a time shortly before the process is implemented in the survey's field period (e.g., typically late in the second week).

Role Playing

Role-playing opportunities also should be built into the part of the training that deals with general work expectations. For example, interviewers can practice trying to gain cooperation from a reluctant respondent whose role can be played by the person conducting the training session. Role playing is also an effective way to illustrate any challenging *skip patterns* in a PAPI questionnaire or to practice proper probing techniques with open-end items.

Role playing allows for the active involvement of interviewers in the training session, in contrast to the passive training they receive when the trainer is talking, while watching a demonstration tape, or while reading the training manual. As such, most interviewers appear to especially enjoy this part of training.

CATI

With CATI, role playing can be combined also with practice with the computer system. However, before an interviewer can benefit from role-playing training on CATI, separate training sessions must be held to familiarize interviewers with the operations of the CATI system (hardware and software) they will be using. Regardless of which system is used, the interviewer must understand that her or his "primary job is interviewing, not operating a CATI system" (House & Nicholls, 1988, p. 427).

In training interviewers on CATI, it is beneficial to explain how CATI is expected to improve interviewing and thereby lower interviewer-related error (see Groves, 1989, pp. 377-378; Lavrakas, 1991; also see Chapter 1). For example, CATI greatly aids with skip patterns (branching), items that have information that needs to be supplied from previous answers given by the respondent, and items that require random variation in order or wording (see House & Nicholls, 1988). Training should leave interviewers with a clear understanding that the purpose in employing CATI is to improve data quality (i.e., reduced measurement error), even though it has been found to have a slightly higher per interview cost than PAPI, due in part to interviews taking a bit longer to complete (Catlin & Ingram, 1988).

Thus, with CATI systems, it is not enough to train interviewers merely to be technically competent with the hardware and software. Training should also instill in them an understanding of the potential value of this technological advance to improve data quality and other aspects of reducing total survey error.

Explaining the Supervisory System

The part of training addressing general work expectations should also explain the supervisory system that will be employed to monitor interviewing quality (see Chapter 6). This should help reduce potential conflicts between interviewers and supervisors that may arise because of interviewers not understanding the responsibilities of supervisors vis-à-vis interviewers.

For purposes of illustration, differences in the role of the supervisor in face-to-face interviewing and in telephone interviewing can be compared. Emphasis here should be on the high degree of supervision that centralized telephone interviewing affords and how it relates to minimizing total survey error—in particular, measurement error. Furthermore, it should be noted that there appears to be less interviewer-related error in centralized telephone surveys than with in-person surveys (Tucker, 1983).

Interviewers should be reminded of the structured routine they will be expected to follow—call-sheets will be assigned to them, specific disposition codes will be used, the number dialed must be verified, a selection procedure will single out one eligible person per household, and so on—and that it is the supervisor's responsibility to see that this routine is observed. Interviewers should be told also of the many ways that supervisors check the quality of their interviewing; for example, completed questionnaires should be immediately turned in to supervisors for review to immediately *validate* their completeness. Also, a centralized telephone bank ideally will allow supervisory personnel to listen to all aspects of the interviewing process. Interviewers should understand that this occurs primarily so supervisors can provide interviewers with constructive feedback to try to lessen total survey error. Finally, interviewers should be aware that a small proportion of their completions may be chosen for verification by supervisory personnel (see Chapter 6).

In explaining to interviewers why this intensive level of monitoring is desirable, the trainer should link it to the need professionally to guarantee the survey's sponsor that high quality interviewing occurs. It should not be made to appear to interviewers that they are not trusted, but rather that supervisors will be assisting them do the best possible interviewing.

Interviewer Productivity

Interviewers should also understand what is expected of them from the standpoint of productivity. A basic measure of interviewer productivity is to compare the number of properly completed interviews attained per interviewing session with the number of refusals (and partials) the interviewer experiences. I believe a goal for which interviewers should be trained to strive is to achieve at least four completions for every one refusal or partial, thereby yielding a response rate of 80% or higher. This is essentially similar to average response rates for interviewers at Michigan's Survey Research Center (Groves, 1989, p. 195). When sampling is done primarily in urban areas this ratio may be unrealistically high, yet it remains a desirable goal for interviewers to set for themselves. Interviewers should be told this, with an emphasis on what *properly completed* means, and should be provided an explanation of why refusals and noncontacts can add to total survey error with the potential of undermining a survey's validity.

In discussing productivity with interviewers the trainer should note that the average number of completions that can be expected per hour will depend upon the length of the questionnaire and the productivity of the sampling pool in reaching eligible respondents (see Chapter 2). For the purpose of comparison, my own experience with RDD telephone surveys indicates that when a questionnaire averages 25-30 minutes in length the average number of completions per hour is about one. With questionnaires in the 15-20 minute range, completions per hour average about two, or a little less. With shorter questionnaires hourly output increases inversely.

Interviewers should understand what the surveyor reasonably expects in terms of hourly output, especially if wages are tied, in part, to completions (as discussed later).

Interviewers also should understand that daily tallies of their productivity are taken and that their refusal rate is compared to their completion rate. Interviewers must recognize that if they consistently receive too many refusals, their continued tenure is unlikely as this increases the survey's nonresponse rate and, thereby, may increase total survey error.

Finally, the speed at which call-sheets are processed should be mentioned. Interviewers are not expected to rush from one dialing to another, but they should understand that there should be no appreciable delays between dialings.

Depending upon the resources committed to supervision, the quality of interviewing can be assessed through the use of a monitoring form developed expressly for this purpose (see Chapter 6). If deployed, the form should be reviewed during the general training so that interviewers also will understand the criteria that are used to judge interviewing quality—for example, the extent to which questions are read exactly as worded, the frequency with which the interviewer offers unneeded comments, and so on.

Explaining to interviewers what is expected of them in terms of quantity should never diminish the primary importance of quality. But most survey endeavors have tight budgets and are constantly faced with the practical realities of balancing quality and quantity.

Payment and Other Employment Practices

The final points that should be discussed by the trainer regarding general work practices and expectancies deal with the specific procedures used by whoever is conducting the survey: What employment forms should be filled out, how will work schedules be assigned, what is the attendance policy, how and when will interviewers be paid for their work (or credited, in the case of unpaid interviewers), and so on?

Payment is a critical issue that deserves its own discussion. Psychologically, the manner in which interviewers are paid ideally should reflect the expectancies that are held of them. The standard approach to paying interviewers is with an hourly wage. The reasoning behind the practice of paying by the hour, regardless of productivity, is its bureaucratic convenience and a belief that it is the best way to emphasize quality over mere quantity. The latter is based on the assumption that if interviewers were paid on a piecemeal basis (per completed interview) they would be reinforced to go as fast as possible, thus sacrificing quality.

Although this is the reasoning held by many survey professionals, I believe it denies the ability of a highly structured supervisory system to assure quality interviewing under individualized modes of payment that directly reward merit. My experience in the past 15 years with telephone surveys leads me to recommend consideration of a mixed mode of payment, in which the majority of income earned by interviewers comes from a standard hourly wage, but in which a proportion of their wages is also based on their productivity. In general a 3:1 balance seems to be a good one; for example, interviewers might be paid a base of $6.00 per hour and earn an additional $2.00 per hour, on average, based on their own productivity.

Psychologically, this mixed mode reflects the fact that many surveys are not conducted by well-funded survey organizations that can afford the luxury of employing interviewers who may be slow but do high-quality interviewing. Although all interviewing must be of acceptable quality, the mixed mode payment recognizes that many very capable interviewers often average relatively more completions per hour, with fewer refusals, than interviewers with less capability in following standardized interviewing procedures. By providing a monetary increment linked to a completion-refusal formula, I believe a more equitable reward structure is instituted.

NUSL has used this mixed mode of payment of interviewers, on occasion, for the past 10 years, and has never received a complaint that it is unfair from the scores of interviewers who have been paid under this system. Granted, the mixed mode approach to payment requires more record keeping than with a mere standard hourly wage, but it reflects the individual attention that I believe is consistent with expectations of interviewing quality.

In sum, interviewers should be explicitly trained to recognize that they can earn a good income provided they conform to the standards of those responsible for conducting a survey. High-quality telephone interviewing is not easy work; as such, good interviewers appear to appreciate the opportunity to have their earnings partly reflect their job performance.

Interviewers who are familiar with general procedures and expectations need not attend the first part of training for every survey, although it is prudent to have even the most experienced ones attend occasionally as a "refresher" experience. Although some experienced interviewers may balk at this, the importance of occasional review of standardized interviewing procedures is highlighted by findings that experience level of interviewers is basically unrelated to accuracy in reading questions (see Groves, 1989, pp. 383-385).

A final point: Interviewers should recognize (and ideally internalize) that they are responsible for leaving all persons whom they contact with a good impression of surveys. In other words, I believe interviewers should feel a sense of professional responsibility to the survey research enterprise to avoid leaving respondents with a bad taste for telephone surveys.

Training for a Specific Survey

Regardless of how often experienced interviewers attend general training, all interviewers must be trained in the particulars of each new survey. Generally, this second part of training should be structured as follows:

1. an explanation of the purpose of the survey;
2. a review of how the sampling pool was generated and how telephone numbers will be processed;
3. an explanation of the use of the introduction/selection sheet;
4. a review of fallback statements;
5. an explanation of the refusal report form (RRF), if one is used; and
6. a detailed explanation of the questionnaire, including practice in its use.

With CATI, any atypical software sequences should be explained clearly and ample time allotted for on-line practice.

A standard approach to follow is to have a survey-specific interviewer training packet for each person who will be working on a survey. This packet contains examples of the forms that will be used in the survey and written instructions to supplement what is explained verbally in the training session.

Purpose of Survey

By understanding and appreciating the purpose of the survey, interviewers should be more likely to believe in the importance of the data they are gathering. This belief can provide interviewers with a sense of confidence that comes from knowing they are engaged in a meaningful enterprise that someone (the survey's sponsor) cares about. As such, it is recommended that the sponsor attend this part of training and participate in an explanation of the survey's purpose. Not only is the sponsor most knowledgeable about this, but, as important, it provides interviewers an opportunity to meet the person for whom they are ultimately working.

The explanation of purpose given to interviewers need not be too detailed. Furthermore, it should not be decided arbitrarily whether specific research hypotheses (if there are any) should be shared with interviewers. If there is a chance that this type of knowledge may bias data by creating expectations on the part of interviewers, it is prudent not to provide it. On the other hand, it can undermine interviewers' ability to persuade reluctant respondents if the interviewers are too uninformed about the survey's purpose.

Sampling Pool and Call-Sheet

Interviewers should understand, in nonacademic terms, what target population is being studied and how the sampling pool represents that population; for example, is it RDD or list-based? The call-sheet that will be used in the survey should be discussed, particularly noting the number of callbacks that will be used for hard-to-reach respondents and any differences from other call-sheets interviewers may have used. Interviewers should be reminded that they are expected to fill out the date, time, and their ID number *before* each dialing (with some CATI systems, the software does this automatically). Specific disposition codes should be reviewed, but discussed in detail only if they are ones with which interviewers are not already familiar.

Introduction/Selection Sheet

An explanation of the introduction/selection sheet then should be presented. Depending upon the complexity of the selection procedure, the trainer may choose to engage some interviewers in a form of role playing, taking on the part of potential respondents and having several different interviewers (one at a time) use the selection procedure. This helps to highlight difficult parts of the selection procedure, if there are any, and reinforces for interviewers that they need practice in its use before the next part of training or before beginning to interview.

Fallback Statements

Because questions from gatekeepers and potential respondents are most likely to arise while the interviewer is using the introduction/selection sheet, it is at this point in training that specific fallback statements should be discussed. The nuances of each of these standardized responses should be noted. Interviewers should be reminded to practice using these statements before starting to interview.

Refusal Report Form

If a survey will employ a refusal report form it should be reviewed prior to explaining the questionnaire. To the extent that the RRF is different from those with which interviewers are experienced, these differences should be highlighted. It is wise to remind interviewers of the value of the information recorded on the RRF and how these forms will be used in refusal conversion attempts.

Questionnaire

The trainer then should proceed through the questionnaire, item by item, reading most, if not all, items in their entirety (including the response options) to provide an example to all interviewers on the use of the questionnaire. Skip patterns that require interviewers to ask different items depending on certain responses need special attention, especially with PAPI where the skipping is done manually. If open-end items are included in the questionnaire, the trainer must explain the type and amount of detail that is expected that interviewers will write down *legibly*. (With PAPI, the amount of space that is physically provided on a page to record open-end answers structures an expectancy on the part of interviewers regarding how much should be written.) Probing instructions specific to certain open-end items must be explained also.

After a detailed review of the questionnaire, role playing should be used. Interviewers should be separated into groupings of five or fewer and assigned to practice the questionnaire with a supervisor taking on the role of a respondent. Practice with the questionnaire can proceed in a round-robin fashion, following skip patterns depending on the responses given by the supervisor. (Interviewers typically enjoy this part of training sessions as it allows for their active involvement.) In general, role playing should last approximately 20-60 minutes depending upon the length and complexity of the questionnaire. It is the purpose of role playing not to make interviewers entirely expert with the questionnaire, but rather to increase their knowledge of the instrument and to bring out any uncertainties they may have about its use.

Ending the Training Session

This survey-specific training session, which typically will last 2-4 hours, should conclude with a review of what was covered and with a reminder of the importance of the interviewer becoming very familiar with all the materials in the training packet. The trainer should also allude to the nature of any other presurvey or on-the-job training that will be done. At the conclusion of this session it is useful also to review the interviewing schedule.

PRESURVEY PRACTICE
AND ON-THE-JOB TRAINING

Although training sessions play an important role in informing interviewers about all aspects of the survey process, the best training occurs via actual interviewing, whether in the form of presurvey practice or on-the-job training. Those familiar with telephone surveys know that interviewers typically take one or two interviewing sessions to "hit their stride" with each new survey. Recognizing this, an ideal (albeit costly) approach to training is to have at least one practice session of actual interviewing for each interviewer before the interviewer starts to generate completions that count toward the survey's final sample size. (Telephone numbers used in practice should be a random subset of the sampling pool so as not to bias the final sample.)

When a surveyor can afford to take this approach, it further serves to screen those interviewers who are likely to gather the best quality data, especially from among a new group of interviewers. A final employment decision can be withheld until after each new interviewer has completed at least one practice session. For example, missing a scheduled practice session may be a warning sign of the interviewer's potential unreliability.

In practice sessions (and actual work sessions) it is the supervisor's responsibility to provide constant feedback to interviewers about all aspects of their work (see Chapter 6). This is done by checking completions immediately as they occur, reviewing call-sheets that have not led to completions, and spending as much time as possible listening to ongoing interviewing. If resources permit, interviewers can be tape-recorded (providing respondents give their permission), which can aid supervisory personnel in providing feedback pegged to specific problems that the tape can illustrate (see Fowler & Mangione, 1985). Because this is very demanding work for a supervisor, a maximum of 8-10 interviewers should be employed for every one supervisor. During practice sessions and in the early stages of a demanding survey, even this ratio is high, so it is ideal to maintain a 4:1 or 5:1 interviewer-to-supervisor ratio at these times.

Supervisors and the field director should review constantly the ability of new interviewers and make a decision whether or not to continue a

person on a particular survey. Periodic reviews of interviewer performance should continue throughout the field period. Whenever necessary,
supervisors or the field director should arrange for an interviewer who
is not meeting standards to discuss the improvements needed by the
interviewer.

For larger survey efforts, the use of a structured individualized feedback
mechanism to convey information to interviewers about their performance should be considered. The printed feedback might be produced on a
monthly basis and could reinforce on-the-job training by reviewing areas
in which improvement has been made or in which improvement is still
needed.

Theoretically, on-the-job training never stops. It always remains the
supervisor's responsibility to monitor the quality of interviewing and thus
to provide ongoing feedback to all interviewers, regardless of their seniority. When this is done by skilled, conscientious supervisors a group of
highly skilled interviewers should result: one whose energetic approach
to their work does not bias or otherwise compromise the quality of the
survey data.

TOTAL SURVEY ERROR
AND THE INTERVIEWER

Despite the resources a survey enterprise commits to hiring and training
interviewers, at least some interviewer-related error (i.e., variation and/or
bias in survey data associated with the people who served as interviewers)
is likely to occur, even in the best of telephone surveys. As such, a surveyor
is well-advised to consider other operational factors and statistical inves-
tigations related to the size of the error due to interviewers. For example,
the more interviewers that are used on a particular survey, the lower should
be interviewer-related measurement variance, although interviewer-related
measurement bias may increase (see Groves, 1989, p. 315). Of course, the
practical matter of cost places real limits on the number of paid interviewers a surveyor can commit to a survey, as discussed in Chapter 6.

There are several statistical techniques that allow a surveyor to estimate
the size of the variation in specific questionnaire items due to interviewer
effects. Kish (1962) explained the use of *rho* (intraclass correlation
coefficient) as a measure of the variance in a survey question associated
with interviewers (see also Fowler & Mangione, 1990; Groves, 1989,
p. 318). Wolter (1985) discussed the use of "jackknife" variance calcula-

tion methods whereby all the interviews of one interviewer at a time are dropped from calculations of survey statistics (such as means); the resulting variances in the statistics are then used to estimate the size of the interviewer-related effects. The advanced reader is also encouraged to review Stokes and Ming-Yih's (1988) work on modeling interviewer effects and Groves (1989, pp. 360-381).

Throughout this edition, I have alluded to the distinction between trying to reduce total survey error and trying to measure its magnitude. The two perspectives complement each other in quality survey work. In terms of interviewer-related error, there is only so much that reasonably can be done to reduce its existence. Thus, surveyors should consider trying to estimate its magnitude to enhance their understanding of their survey findings.

EXERCISES

Exercise 5.1: Produce a display ad for hiring interviewers at a telephone survey organization. (Optional: Include graphics in the display).

Exercise 5.2: Summarize the differences between conducting a telephone survey with paid interviewers and conducting it with unpaid volunteers.

Exercise 5.3: Write the dialogue of a scenario illustrating the possible exchange between a respondent who is very reluctant to participate in a survey and a highly persuasive (but polite) interviewer.

Exercise 5.4: In outline form, plan a 3-hour survey-specific training session that would include 20 new (paid) interviewers and 20 previously employed interviewers. Indicate the time (in minutes) you would allocate to each part of the session.

Exercise 5.5: As an in-class project, have class members assemble in small groups and practice the use of a telephone survey questionnaire via role playing.

6

Supervision II:
Structuring Supervisory Work

This text has stressed the opportunity afforded by telephone surveys to reduce total survey error through intensive supervision during the entire data collection process. Chapter 3 explained how a highly routinized system for processing the telephone numbers in a sampling pool may be structured. The importance of supervisory personnel, in particular the person who controls the sampling pool, was discussed. Chapter 5 explained the role of the trainer in interviewer training sessions and the role of supervisors in on-the-job training and in monitoring interviewing sessions.

The present chapter focuses in more detail on supervisory responsibilities throughout the data collection process and provides further elaboration on other supervisory tasks in quality telephone surveys. It touches upon the role of the survey's field director and identifies other administrative tasks that provide a smooth-flowing telephone survey operation.

Although it may not be obvious to the reader, it is quite possible that one person could assume all (or at least most) of the supervisory responsibilities for a telephone survey. For example, for nearly 10 years I taught a 2-week unit on public opinion polling in an advanced undergraduate journalism class three times each year. As part of this unit students participated as interviewers in an RDD telephone survey (final sample size of about 400 completions) using a systematic selection of respondents within households with up to three callbacks for hard-to-reach respondents. The questionnaire averaged about 20 closed-end items. Within a 10-day period, I generated the sampling pool, developed the questionnaire with the students, trained them as interviewers, scheduled and set up each interviewing session, supervised all interviewing, controlled the processing of the sampling pool, edited and keyed the data, and performed a fairly robust set of statistical analyses that were reported back to the class.

Although most users of this text are unlikely to have to assume all these responsibilities, some may need to do even more, as in the case of a graduate student who is gathering thesis data via a telephone survey, who may also have to conduct all of the interviewing. In other cases, a researcher will hire a survey organization to conduct a telephone survey or may need to consider setting up a temporary organizational structure to complete a specific survey project. In these instances it is useful to be familiar with operational structures for centralized telephone surveys and their costs (see Bass & Tortora, 1988; Berry & O'Rourke, 1988; Frey, 1989, pp. 185-199; Groves, 1989, pp. 526-550).

Here, a major consideration is whether or not operations will include CATI capability. With CATI there is a lot more investment required than merely purchasing computer software and hardware. For example, to be adequately implemented, CATI requires at least 33%-50% more square feet of office space than is needed to support the same level of PAPI interviewing. CATI also requires a more substantial investment in furnishings and (more important) in administrative staff for software programming and hardware maintenance. Despite its technological attractiveness, CATI is not a panacea and should be implemented (or migrated to) carefully, as discussed in Chapter 1. Too little is known at present to be able to identify with great confidence those surveys for which a CATI deployment should have a superior cost-benefit ratio over PAPI (see Catlin & Ingram, 1988). (In this case, *benefit* refers to the size of the total survey error.) Thus, the interested reader is encouraged to follow the evolving literature on when to use CATI and when to use PAPI.

Regardless of the operational structure and of whether or not CATI is used, there are many basic supervisory tasks that must be routinely performed to assure quality telephone surveys. It is these tasks that are discussed in this chapter.

STAFFING AND SCHEDULING
INTERVIEWING SESSIONS

There are many duties for which supervisory personnel are responsible at times when no interviewing session is scheduled. In fact, if these duties were not performed, interviewing would not be possible or, at best, would be highly disorganized. The first of these responsibilities has to do with staffing and scheduling interviewing sessions. Most of the discussion presented in this section concerning staffing assumes that interviewers will be paid for their work, but some of the considerations also apply to interviewers who are unpaid.

Staffing

In large survey organizations there will be a field director who assumes responsibility for hiring and staffing interviewers. In smaller operations someone in a supervisory capacity will take this on. To determine how many interviewers will be needed to staff the survey's field period, one must take into account:

1. how productive each interviewer is likely to be during each work session;
2. the number of times each interviewer will work per week;
3. the average number of interviewers who will work per session;
4. the number of interviewing sessions that will be held each week; and
5. the total number of completions that are needed.

For example, if a survey used RDD sampling and the questionnaire took about 15 minutes to administer, interviewers might be expected to produce two completions per hour, or eight completions in a typical 4-hour work session. If there were six work sessions scheduled each week with 10 telephones available for interviewing, then about 480 completions could be expected per week. Depending on the average number of times interviewers worked each week, one could estimate how many interviewers would be required to keep telephones fully staffed. The greater the total number of completions needed for the survey, the more likely one would need to adjust (increase) the number of interviewers hired to allow for poor attendance and attrition.

If, in this example, the desired number of completions was 2,400, approximately 5 weeks of interviewing would be needed at full staff. If interviewers worked, on average, three sessions per week, then each interviewer over the 5-week field period would be expected to produce about 120 completions (i.e., eight completions per session multiplied by three sessions per week multiplied by 5 weeks). Strictly speaking, the survey would require 20 interviewers to complete the 2,400 completions. However, it would be prudent to hire and train 10%-30% more interviewers to allow for interviewer attrition and less than perfect attendance.

As noted earlier, a relatively larger number of interviewers employed on a survey is associated theoretically with lower interviewer-related variance (Groves, 1989). But if taken to an extreme, this approach to trying to reduce total survey error would not be cost-effective. Groves (pp. 62-72, 365-374) provides an advanced discussion on the optimal number of interviewers (and supervisors) from a cost-benefit standpoint. Our knowledge in this field is not yet so precise that one can assert the exact number of interviewers that should be scheduled on a project. Rather, the field director should be able to calculate a reasonable range of needed interviewers—one that balances practical needs and costs with total survey error considerations.

The best place to advertise for high-caliber interviewers is on or near college and university campuses. This will attract students, spouses of students and employees, and residents of the communities in which these institutions are located. Although students often make good interviewers, a common disadvantage to employing them is their attendance unreliability due to their academic commitments and life-styles. Thus I strongly recommend that interviewers not be hired exclusively from the student population if surveys are to be completed within the most cost-effective field period.

As mentioned in Chapter 5, one of the most important attributes for making a hiring decision is an interviewer's telephone presence. Therefore, the person doing the hiring should initially interview applicants via telephone and rate their voices and styles of speaking along dimensions deemed relevant to good telephone interviewing. These include confidence, pleasantness, clarity, speed, volume, intelligence, and maturity. To facilitate this rating, the application form should ask some open-end questions that get the applicant to talk.

Scheduling

After preliminary staffing decisions have been made and training has been conducted, scheduling must be finalized. For surveys of the general public, Sunday through Thursday evenings and Saturday afternoons are the best time to reach most potential respondents, although every sampling area has its own idiosyncratic patterns of when residents are more likely to be/not be at home (see Frey, 1989, pp. 232-235). For example, in areas of the South, many residents go to church meetings on Sunday night.

If 4-hour interviewing sessions are planned, then 5:00-9:00 p.m. or 5:30-9:30 p.m. is recommended for evening sessions (see Weeks, Jones, Folsom, & Benrud, 1980; Weeks, Kulka, & Pierson, 1987). Even though this overlaps with the dinner hour, skilled interviewers should have no problem arranging a callback at a more convenient time. If a survey is sampling across time zones interviewing hours should be adjusted accordingly.

Sunday through Thursday evenings normally have constant levels of productivity, with the exception of Mondays during the fall months when a proportion of the public seems to not want to be bothered when professional football is on television. Friday and Saturday evenings are the least productive since these are the nights when most social entertaining is done. Furthermore, interviewers and supervisors are least likely to want to work on these evenings.

Saturday daytime from 11:00 a.m. to 4:00 p.m. is a fairly productive time for interviewing in most areas, despite the fact that callbacks are likely because designated respondents often are doing weekend chores or errands. Of note, experience suggests that many potential respondents who are unavailable during weekday evenings may be reached on Saturday. During certain times of the year, however, Saturday and Sunday afternoons will show a decrease in productivity because of televised sports events.

There will be other occasions when normal evening sessions should be canceled because of some television special that is likely to be watched by a substantial proportion of the public (e.g., the Super Bowl). Not only will productivity be low at these times, but adamant refusals appear more likely to be experienced than otherwise would occur had certain households been called on another occasion; furthermore, data quality may decrease during these times, thereby increasing measurement error.

Depending on the allowable length of the survey's field period, daytime interviewing during weekdays should be scheduled. Afternoon hours, 1:00-5:00 p.m., are generally preferable to morning hours. Daytime interviewing on weekdays will help clean RDD sampling pools of business and nonworking numbers, although many designated respondents will be unavailable because they are working. Experience shows that interviewer productivity (in terms of completions per hour) in RDD surveys during weekday afternoons can be expected to be about 60%-80% that of evenings. One advantage to daytime sessions is that elderly respondents appear less unsettled by a stranger calling, more alert, and more cooperative. In addition, parents who do not work outside the home appear more relaxed without their school-aged children and/or spouses around. However, a valid sample of adults will not be achieved if only daytime sessions were to be scheduled due to nonresponse (noncontact) error.

With telephone surveys of target populations other than the general public, interviewing will need to be conducted at those times when respondents are most likely to be available. For example, a telephone survey of attorneys or other professionals at their place of employment should concentrate interviewing during weekday daytime hours and allow for many callbacks. A telephone survey of high school students at their homes might concentrate interviewing between 3:00 p.m. and 7:00 p.m. on Mondays through Thursdays. Whatever the particular availability of the population being sampled, interviewing sessions should be targeted to those hours.

Seasonality should also be considered when scheduling a field period. If there is any reason to believe that the focus of the survey may be confounded with the time of the year, explicit consideration should be made for its scheduling. For general population surveys with relatively short field periods, it may be wise not to collect data exclusively during summer months, or in mid- to late-December (see Frey, 1989, p.234). Otherwise, nonresponse is likely to increase because of persons on vacation or other personal priorities (e.g., holiday cooking or shopping).

Once it has been determined when interviewing sessions will be scheduled, sufficient numbers of interviewers need to be slotted to keep available telephones adequately staffed. If after a week of interviewing it is found that at least one telephone is regularly going unused because of poor attendance (and this may happen due to the part-time nature of telephone interviewing), one alternative to consider is "over-booking" interviewers. For example, if 10 telephones are available, one may choose to schedule 11 interviewers for each session, knowing from experience that on most occasions at least one will not attend. This, of course, can create problems when all scheduled interviewers *do* appear.

Depending on how many telephones are used during interviewing sessions, it can be quite time-consuming to schedule interviewers. It is recommended that a person with supervisory experience make these contacts so that judgment can be exercised on the likelihood that the contacted interviewer will, in fact, work those sessions he or she has been scheduled. If attendance has been a problem for a specific interviewer, then a call to schedule work sessions can also serve as a warning about the possible termination of the interviewer's employment.

A final consideration in scheduling occurs with the occasional need to staff interviewing sessions only with interviewers of certain demographic groups (e.g., females). As noted earlier, if interviewers' demographic characteristics are related to the substantive focus of a survey (such as the earlier example of the survey on sexual harassment), consideration must be given to match these interviewer characteristics to the needs of the survey (see Groves, 1989, pp. 398-404). Avoiding this somewhat difficult-to-implement practice would lead to a very likely increase in measurement error. As long as interviewers understand that they are not being discriminated against, but rather that the research requires only certain demographic groups of interviewers to gather data, personnel problems should be held to a minimum.

INTERVIEWING SESSION SETUP

In addition to the need for an effective system for staffing and scheduling interviewers, supervisory personnel also need to set up the centralized telephone location on a daily basis. This needs to be done prior to each interviewing session and assumes certain tasks have been completed since the end of the previous session. Although the exact tasks in which supervisory personnel will need to engage will differ for PAPI versus CATI, there are many more similarities than differences in the two interviewing environments.

When interviewers arrive they should find the interviewing room arranged for them to begin interviewing. Their workstations should be well-lit, clean, and organized; with PAPI surveys, call-sheets, questionnaires, and pencils should await them. Ideally, each telephone and/or CATI work-station will be positioned at its own carrel or booth to enclose interviewers in their own environments. If this type of furniture is not available, interviewing equipment can be located at tables, none of which should have interviewers facing each other.

Before the interviewing room can be fully set up for PAPI sessions, call-sheets from the previous session must be sorted (manually) according to their most recent disposition. Telephones numbers that are still active (e.g., specific callbacks and ring-no-answers) are then interspersed with a small number of untried call-sheets. A sufficient amount of call-sheets to keep interviewers busy for about half the session should be placed at each workstation. With full CATI systems, the software generally can be used to assign telephone numbers to interviewers as needed, using com-puter algorithms to try callbacks at optimal times based on a number's call-history (see Groves, 1989, pp. 196-201).

In most surveys, regardless of PAPI or CATI, telephone numbers generally should be distributed to interviewers in a random manner, so that interviewers work random subsets of the active sampling pool. Further-more, "randomization reinforces equity" (Groves, 1989, p. 362), thereby enhancing interviewer morale. On occasion, supervisory personnel will need to assign specific callbacks to specific interviewers. Interviewers should understand the rationale behind these nonrandom assignments. Even with full CATI systems that automatically assign the sampling pool to interviewers, human intervention occasionally may be needed to make proper assignment decisions about specific numbers.

With PAPI, it is best not to give interviewers too many call-sheets to start with; as needed they can get more from the supervisor, thus signaling they are making progress in dialing numbers. Another reason it is prefer-able to have supervisory personnel manually control the flow of call-sheets in PAPI telephone surveys is that interviewers, if allowed to choose call-sheets for themselves, will often display idiosyncratic behaviors that may bias sampling and/or increase interviewer-related error.

With experience, the person responsible for setting up PAPI sessions will learn how many call-sheets the average interviewer can be expected to process during the first half of the session. This will depend upon the length of the questionnaire and the efficiency of the sampling pool. With longer questionnaires and/or a more efficient sampling pool, proportionately more of an interviewer's time will be spent interviewing, rather than dialing numbers, thus fewer call-sheets will be processed each hour. In contrast, with a shorter questionnaire and/or a less efficient sampling pool, proportionately more time will be spent cleaning the sample of ineligible telephone numbers and with noncontacts, thus more call-sheets will be processed per hour. In the case of PAPI and CATI surveys that employ long questionnaires (20 minutes or more), the supervisor should inform interviewers toward the end of the session when to stop trying to get one more completion. If not otherwise told by the supervisor, interviewers have a tendency to stop calling sooner than necessary when they are working with a long questionnaire, thus inflating total survey costs (see Groves, 1989, p. 491).

With PAPI, it is good practice to place fewer questionnaires at each work station than the average number the interviewer will complete in the entire work session. This will reinforce for interviewers that they have made progress during the work session because they have used all the questionnaires at their workstations and will need to request a few more from the supervisor.

Depending on the type of telephone equipment used for interviewing, a certain amount of cleaning will be required prior to each session. At a minimum, each workstation should be vacuumed or dusted prior to interviewers' arrival. If telephones have individualized headsets, interviewers can keep their own earpieces clean. The microphone on most types of headsets does not come into contact with an interviewer's mouth and should only occasionally need cleaning. But if hand-held telephone receivers are used, the entire external surface of the receiver should be cleaned with a nontoxic solvent prior to each session. At least once a week, each receiver should be disassembled and cleaned inside.

Cleanliness in the work setting is not merely a courtesy to interviewers; it reinforces order and helps keep interviewers healthy. Given the importance of interviewers' voices, colds and other respiratory ailments greatly impair their ability to do good telephone interviewing. Given that unreliable attendance is a frequent problem with many part-time telephone interviewers, it behooves supervisory personnel not to contribute to interviewers' potential health problems.

A final aspect of preparing the interviewing room prior to each session is the inclusion of interviewer-specific information in their work folders. There should be a file cabinet or set of mailboxes near where interviewing occurs that contains a separate folder for each interviewer. After interviewers sign in, they retrieve their folders to review any new information before beginning to call. With this system, supervisory personnel can assign partial PAPI questionnaires to specific interviewers for reprocessing. Memos to all interviewers can be put in folders, as can notes about specific problems from the previous time an interviewer worked. If something more serious needs to be discussed with a supervisor prior to an interviewer continuing to interview, a message can be placed in the folder instructing the interviewer to see the supervisor. With some CATI systems an "electronic folder" can be maintained that interviewers log onto before starting to interview.

It will help convey a positive message about the professional quality of interviewing that is expected if interviewers arrive at a centralized location that looks (and is) organized. Supervisory or other administrative personnel, as opposed to interviewers, will not only set up the work sessions more uniformly, but by relieving interviewers of these tasks it allows interviewers to concentrate on high-quality interviewing, not "housekeeping."

SUPERVISING INTERVIEWING SESSIONS IN PAPI AND CATI SURVEYS

As exhausting as quality telephone interviewing can be, the demands on supervisors of interviewing sessions are even greater. It is these individuals' responsibility to ensure the integrity of sampling and the quality of the data that are gathered. For these reasons energetic and skilled persons should be employed in supervisory positions and paid accordingly— approximately three times the minimum wage, which in 1992 equated to nearly $13.00 per hour.

Persons who have had graduate school training in the social sciences often have the qualities desired of good supervisors: They are intelligent, are willing to work hard in a highly structured setting, and usually have a good appreciation of scientific research and the role of quality sampling and quality interviewing within the endeavor in reducing total survey error.

In general, considering both costs and data quality, an optimal ratio should be one supervisor for every 8 to 10 experienced interviewers (see Groves, 1989, pp. 61-62). When a supervisor is responsible for more than 10 interviewers, time demands become so intense that it is difficult for quality supervision to occur. However, it neither is cost-effective nor often necessary to limit the number of interviewers for which a supervisor is responsible to fewer than eight. An exception is with new interviewers or at the start of a field period, when it is prudent to maintain closer to a 1:5 supervisor/interviewer ratio.

It is the responsibility of the field director to supervise the supervisors. This includes their hiring, their training, and a constant review of on-the-job performance. Supervisors should know that the field director may attend an interviewing session unannounced to assess how well supervisors are executing their responsibilities. These responsibilities, which will vary somewhat from survey to survey, are addressed below.

Creating a Productive Interviewing Environment

Supervisors are responsible for maintaining the quality of the interviewing that occurs during their sessions, and interviewers should clearly perceive that the supervisor feels and displays this responsibility. It is advised that supervisors report to their sessions at least 30 minutes before interviewers to check that all is ready for the session to start (and to make it ready if it is not) and to prepare themselves for the arrival of interviewers.

The authority a supervisor exhibits in her or his sessions should be confident, fair, consistent, and tempered with a pleasant, yet not overly friendly demeanor. Constructive criticism should be provided to interviewers in a manner that enhances the likelihood that the interviewer will take it to heart and not reject it, as might be the case if it were conveyed in too harsh, negative, or embarrassing a fashion.

Supervisors should themselves be trained to determine the level at which an interviewing-related problem occurs (Cannell & Oksenberg, 1988). It may be that an interviewer has yet to receive adequate training and, therefore, is unfamiliar with proper techniques. It may be that the interviewer knows what to do, but not exactly how to operationalize it; or, that the interviewer knows how it is supposed to be done, but lacks the skill/ability to do it properly. Unless the supervisor can judge accurately the level of the problem, she or he is not likely to be able to propose an effective solution to the interviewer.

Validating Completions

As mentioned in Chapter 5, upon completion of an interview in a PAPI survey each interviewer should be instructed to quickly, yet carefully check over the questionnaire and then immediately submit it to the supervisor. The supervisor, in turn, should inspect the entire question-naire, item-by-item, to *validate* that answers were recorded for all items that should have been asked and that all open-end questions have answers written legibly. To be able to do this accurately and quickly the supervisor must be completely familiar with the questionnaire.

In CATI there is no paper trail for supervisors to work with to perform questionnaire validation; rather, it is assumed that the software provides an acceptable surrogate for validation. Of note, supervisors in CATI environments sometimes report that they "lose the feel" of progress within the interviewing session compared to their experiences with PAPI (see Berry & O'Rourke, 1988, p. 473). (This is another area that will await further study to determine the differential advantages and disadvantages of CATI versus PAPI.)

Unless the supervisor is involved in the resolution of a problem or in answering a question for an interviewer, validation of completions should be the supervisor's first priority in PAPI surveys. The purpose of this priority is to identify problems as soon as possible after they occur. The supervisor can then immediately discuss the remedy with the interviewer before the problem happens again. Many times, a problem can be resolved without the interviewer having to call back a respondent. However, in instances where critical information is missing entirely, the supervisor should instruct the interviewer to call the respondent back immediately to gather the missing data.

Once a PAPI questionnaire has been validated by the supervisor as being properly completed, the supervisor should initial the attached call-sheet to allow for easy identification of who did the validation. The field director should occasionally revalidate completions to check the atten-tiveness of supervisors. Furthermore, when PAPI questionnaires are later edited/coded before they are keyed into machine-readable form, problems that are detected can be traced back easily to the supervisor on duty during the interviewing session in which the completion occurred.

As noted above, the rapport that supervisors develop with interviewers will affect the quality of data produced. There must be constant verbal and/or written feedback to interviewers, especially during the early part of a field period when on-the-job training is critical. The manner in which a supervisor provides feedback should be timely and direct, yet tactful. An interviewer should never be embarrassed by a supervisor in front of other interviewers. This can be avoided if the supervisor writes a note to the interviewer either explaining a minor problem or requesting to speak with the interviewer before the interviewer goes on to another interview. (With some CATI systems the supervisor is able to communicate on-line with interviewers.) In the extreme, supervisors must have the authority and exercise the discretion to stop an interviewer from interviewing for the remainder of a work session if a problem has occurred that the interviewer appears unable or unwilling to correct.

Although it is unreasonable to expect perfection on the part of interviewers and supervisors, a supervisor who concentrates while validating PAPI questionnaires should allow very few interviewing mistakes to slip past. Similarly, when interviewers recognize that their completions are carefully validated it reinforces their attentiveness to conducting interviews in an accurate manner.

For PAPI surveys that employ a refusal report form, a similar system of validating completed RRFs should be instituted: The interviewer should immediately turn in the call-sheet with the attached RRF to the supervisor, who, in turn, should check it for completeness and provide immediate feedback to the interviewer if there is a problem with the manner in which the RRF was completed.

Monitoring Ongoing Interviews

Whenever possible, a telephone survey should use a centralized bank of telephones with equipment that allows the supervisor's telephone to monitor all interviewers' lines. There are special telephones that can monitor ongoing interviews without the interviewer or respondent being aware of it (although there was 1992 legislation proposed in the U.S. Senate that would make this illegal). This also can be done if the supervisor's desk is equipped with a regular telephone that ties into each access line used by interviewers. In this later case the supervisor disconnects the mouthpiece before cutting into the line. When this happens the interviewer (but usually not the respondent) will be aware that the supervisor is listening. Although this may create some disadvantages (e.g., a slight drop in volume on the line), one advantage is that interviewers are certain that the quality of their interviewing is being assessed.

With CATI surveys, monitoring ongoing interviews becomes a supervisor's primary responsibility, since the supervisor does not have completion-validation responsibilities as is the case with PAPI. With PAPI, monitoring ongoing interviews should be a secondary, but nevertheless high supervisory responsibility. Regardless of CATI or PAPI, monitoring can be done formally with the use of a structured interviewer monitoring form (IMF) or informally without a structured procedure.

Supervisors need not listen to complete interviews, but rather should systematically apportion their listening, a few minutes at a time, across all interviewers, concentrating more frequently and at longer intervals on less experienced ones. Assignment of monitoring might even be done using probability sampling to choose which interviewer to monitor, at which time, and for how long (see Couper, Holland, & Groves, 1992).

All aspects of interviewer-respondent contact should be monitored: These include the interviewer's use of the introduction, the respondent selection sequence, the fallback statements, and the questionnaire itself. Depending upon available resources, an IMF can be devised and employed by supervisors. An IMF can (a) aid the supervisor by providing documented on-the-job feedback to interviewers; (b) generate interviewer performance data for the field director; and (c) provide the surveyor with a valuable type of data to investigate item-specific interviewer-related measurement error (see Cannell & Oksenberg, 1988; Groves, 1989, pp. 381-389).

Supervisors should pay special attention to ways in which interviewers probe incomplete, ambiguous, or irrelevant responses, and to whether or not interviewers adequately repeat questions and define/clarify terms a respondent may not understand in an unbiased fashion. Supervisors also need to pay close attention to anything the interviewer may be saying or doing (verbally) that might reinforce certain responses patterns that may bias answers. For example, interviewers should never express their own opinions, even when a respondent asks them, "What do you think?" Nor should interviewers fall into the unconscious habit of saying things like "That's too bad," or "I'm glad to hear that."

With some CATI systems, monitoring ongoing interviews includes being able to view the interviewer's interaction with the computer as it happens. This allows the supervisor also to assess the interviewer's accuracy in recording the answers for both closed- and open-end items; that is, most CATI systems will not allow interviewers to enter out-of-range answer-values, but they cannot guard against incorrect, albeit within-range, answers being keyed.

Most supervisors prefer to use an IMF, even a simple one, as it helps to structure their own work during the session. When circumstances do not lend themselves to employing an IMF, supervisors should be trained to apply the same criteria, informally, in judging the adequacy of an interviewer's on-the-job performance.

When the telephone system that is used for interviewing does not allow a supervisor to listen to interviews, the supervisor should walk frequently about the interviewing room, routinely stopping by each interviewer to briefly listen to the interviewer's part of the conversation. Anyone with telephone interviewing experience knows that it is very difficult to fake an interview if an experienced supervisor is both listening to and watching what the interviewer is doing. An experienced supervisor should be able to detect a bogus interview by its pacing and the consistency/ inconsistency of the apparent responses. Thus, although it is preferable to have a telephone system that allows supervisors to listen directly to ongoing interviews, this aspect of the supervisor's responsibilities should occur regardless of the availability of monitoring equipment.

Listening to ongoing interviewing should be more frequent in the early stages of the field period and with new interviewers. At these times, two supervisors may be preferred for every 8-10 interviewers. Monitoring should not be stopped in later stages of the field period, nor should supervisors avoid listening to experienced interviewers. Unless monitoring follows an assigned schedule, supervisors must exercise common sense in allocating their listening time, within the context of whether they are working on a PAPI or CATI survey.

Monitoring Call-Sheet Dispositions

It is also the supervisor's responsibility to oversee the processing of the sampling pool during the interviewing session. Supervisors should occasionally check the manner in which refusals and partials are being recorded by interviewers, as well as how they are using all disposition codes. Again, the supervisor should concentrate this attention on new interviewers. With PAPI surveys the supervisor will work manually with call-sheets to do this. With some full CATI systems many different types of reports can be generated at a supervisor's or the field director's request to show interviewers' progress in processing the sampling pool (see Weeks, 1988, pp. 418-419).

Another consideration regarding the sampling pool concerns recycling certain numbers during the interviewing session. From previous sessions there may be telephone numbers that need to be redialed at a particular time and/or that should be given to a particular interviewer. With some CATI systems the software may be able to accomplish most or all of this task. With PAPI, the supervisor must see that these call-sheets get to the right interviewer at the right time.

There may be times when an interviewer will lack the confidence to call back a respondent from a previous interviewing session to try to complete a partial. In these instances, the supervisor should discuss this reluctance with the original interviewer and then decide whether to reassign the partial to another interviewer.

Solving Problems and Answering Questions

At all times during interviewing sessions supervisors must be trouble-shooters. They must know how to answer interviewers' questions, antici-pate and solve problems, and generally be ready to deal with the unex-pected. Sometimes interpersonal tensions between interviewers will need to be defused. Other times interviewers may become too chatty, thus reduc-ing their productivity. Occasionally a supervisor may need to speak to an unsettled or irate respondent to apologize for a (possible) mistake on the part of an interviewer, or to resolve some uncertainty that the interviewer cannot explain, or simply to listen courteously to a respondent who requests to talk to a supervisor.

When the Sponsor Visits

Survey sponsors have good reason to want to observe the sessions in which their data are gathered. A sponsor pays for the survey and thus is well justified in wanting firsthand experience with how interviewers are using the questionnaire and other survey materials and how respondents are answering. However, sponsors sometimes have very unrealistic expecta-tions about the enthusiasm that respondents display while participating in surveys. The naive sponsor may presume the questionnaire will be inter-esting and important to all respondents and thus automatically assumes it is the fault of interviewers if some respondents sound somewhat un-focused and/or disinterested while responding.

With this and other potential problems related to a sponsor observing ongoing interviewing sessions, the supervisor must be ready to listen to the concerns of the sponsor but should not deviate from standard survey procedures until the field director has changed policy. At no time should supervisors argue with survey sponsors; rather, the sponsor should be asked to discuss any concerns directly with the field director, who will then inform supervisors of any changes that are warranted.

VERIFYING COMPLETED INTERVIEWS

Another supervisory duty is associated with the *verification* of com-pleted surveys. In addition to the supervisor's validation of each comple-tion during the interviewing session, a survey can be budgeted to include verification of a proportion of all completed interviews. (In the case of a survey NUSL conducted in 1990 for a law firm that intended to enter the findings as evidence in a federal trial, the firm hired another organization to verify all 1,600 of our completions.) Verification of completions requires a supervisory-level person to recontact the respondent to verify that the interview took place and, typically, to verify some of the answers recorded by the interviewer.

If ongoing interviewing is rigorously monitored along the lines described in this chapter, verifying completions may be viewed as optional. However, verification is recommended with new interviewers, especially at the beginning of a survey's field period. It is good for interviewers to know that verification occurs, but it is not necessary for them to know how many of their completions are actually verified.

Any completion that does not verify is cause for concern. It does not mean necessarily that the interview was done improperly (e.g., there are times when respondents will unaccountably be reluctant to admit they participated in a survey), but it signals the need to be vigilant in checking the work of a particular interviewer. In PAPI surveys, occasionally a completion will not verify because the interviewer carelessly attached an incorrect call-sheet to the questionnaire, thereby leading to the wrong number being called back at the time of attempted verification.

As in the case of the data produced by IMFs, a surveyor can use data from verification forms to investigate the size of the survey's measurement error and whether it was likely to be interviewer-related or respondent-related.

CONCLUSION

As Fowler (1984) observed, far too little attention has been paid by survey professionals to sources of error associated with the human part of survey data collection. As should be clear from this chapter, and from this edition as a whole, the quality of the sampling that occurs and the data that are gathered in a telephone survey are highly correlated with the quality of the supervision that is implemented.

Many survey organizations, especially commercial ones, appear unwilling to institute a system that stresses and rewards quality telephone interviewing and supervision. The practice (inadvertent though it may be) of underutilizing the opportunities that telephone surveys provide for a rigorous control of data collection is likely to continue until survey sponsors recognize the need to demand higher quality for their money. This was the opinion I expressed when I began working on the first edition of this book in 1984 and, unfortunately, my assessment of the magnitude of the problem is essentially unchanged since that time.

Throughout this edition the procedures that have been explained assume that a surveyor would like to gather high-quality data—findings with relatively low total survey error—at a reasonable cost. As with many things, cutting telephone survey costs most often means cutting quality, thus increasing the likelihood of total survey error. However, poor-quality interviewing and inadequate supervision actually may prove to be more expensive than top-quality work, especially when the quality is so poor as to completely invalidate the data.

Simply stated, money and effort spent to gather poor-quality survey data is money and effort wasted. In contrast, resources committed to support carefully planned and executed surveys that gather high-quality data may pay for themselves many times over.

EXERCISES

Exercise 6.1: Develop a form to screen applicants, via telephone, for positions as telephone interviewers.

Exercise 6.2: Calculate the number of interviewing sessions needed per week and the number of interviewers to employ for the following survey that must be completed in 3 weeks: 1,500 completions; interviewers will average 1.5 completions per hour; interviewing sessions of 3 hours each; eight telephones in the centralized interviewing room; and, interviewers will work an average of four sessions per week.

Exercise 6.3: Write a work description for a newly hired supervisor explaining the supervisory duties that are expected during an interviewing session. Limit the narrative to 500 words or less.

Exercise 6.4: Develop a one-page interviewer monitoring form (IMF) to assess interviewers' use of both closed- and open-end items.

Exercise 6.5: Develop a one-page form that could be used to verify completed interviews; include an introductory spiel for the callback contact with the respondent.

Glossary of Terms

Access line. A telephone line in each sampling unit (e.g., household) with telephone service that is associated with a distinct telephone number. Nontelephone households, by definition, are those without a telephone access line. Households with more than one telephone number are referred to as having multiple access lines.

Added-digit(s). Techniques for generating a sampling pool whereby "seed" numbers are typically chosen from a directory and then fixed or random digit(s) are added to each seed to form a number for the sampling pool. For example, if 869-5025 is chosen from a directory as a seed and the fixed digit, *1*, is added to all seeds, then 869-5026 is entered into the sampling pool.

Advance contact. Contact with a sampled respondent/household via mail or fax prior to having an interviewer call to conduct a telephone interview. The advance contact is meant to "warm up" the respondent to the forthcoming telephone interview by encouraging cooperation, thus decreasing nonresponse.

Bellcore. The unit of AT&T (which in 1992 was located in Morristown, New Jersey) that routinely compiles a computerized data base with information about area codes and telephone prefixes throughout the United States. In 1992 this data base was available for purchase for $400 and contained more than 50,000 records.

Birthday selection methods. Nonintrusive respondent selection techniques that choose one respondent per sampling unit by asking for the person among all eligibles with the last or next birthday. In theory this selection should be a random one, but in practice the techniques do not appear to yield a true random selection.

Callback. The redialing of a telephone number on a different day and/or time from the previous call-attempt. The purpose of callbacks is to reduce the likelihood of nonresponse error due to noncontacts.

Caller ID. A telecommunications option that can be subscribed to in states where it is legal whereby the telephone number of the incoming call is displayed so that the person who is called can see the number from which the call is being placed. The service is thought to be used by some to screen unwanted calls.

Call forwarding. A telecommunications software option that is subscribed to by a minority of households. It allows incoming calls to one telephone number to be forwarded to, and thus answered by, another telephone number. Call forwarding can distort sampling probabilities in telephone surveys.

Call screening. Either through the use of Caller ID or a telephone answering machine, a person can learn who is calling without disclosing to the caller that anyone is there to receive the call. If the person who is called decides not to answer, he or she has effectively screened out the incoming call.

Call-sheet. The separate piece of paper on which is printed each telephone number released from the sampling pool in a PAPI telephone survey. Call-sheets provide the paper-and-pencil approach for controlling a sampling pool in the absence of a full CATI system. Typical information recorded on the call-sheet includes the date, time, and disposition of each dialing, along with the identification number of the interviewer who made each dialing, and any relevant notes. These sheet are called *interviewer report forms* by some survey organizations.

CATI. Computer-Assisted Telephone Interviewing (CATI) refers to those telephone survey operations that have the interviewing and/or the processing of the sampling pool performed with a computer terminal instead of a paper-and-pencil approach. These systems may use the computers to form and control the sampling pool, to prompt interviewers with the introductory spiel and selection procedure, to display the questionnaire item-by-item following proper skip patterns, and to record responses directly into machine-readable data files. CATI is a still-developing technology and its effect on total survey error continues to be studied.

Cold-call. The calling of a potential respondent without first sending advance notification (mail or fax) to alert the person that he or she has been sampled for a telephone survey.

Controller of the sampling pool. The person responsible for releasing telephone numbers from the sampling pool and for making decisions about the final proper disposition of each number that has been released.

Conversion of refusals. The redialing of initial refusals one or more times in order to try to reduce the size of nonresponse by reducing the number of refusals and thereby attempting to increase the external validity (representativeness) of the final sample. Refusal report forms assist in the refusal conversion process.

Coverage error. The portion of total survey error due to not providing every element in the population a nonzero probability of selection. The magnitude of the coverage error is a function of the size of the proportion of the population that was afforded no chance of being sampled and its difference from the proportion of the population that was sampled.

Dialing disposition. The outcome of any dialing attempt of a telephone number released from a sampling pool. The disposition is typically recorded on the call-sheet using a numerical coding system.

Disposition code. The number assigned to a specific kind of dialing outcome (e.g., ring-no-answer, nonworking number, respondent refusal, etc.) that is used to manage the sampling pool.

External validity. The accuracy with which one can generalize survey results from a sample to the population it purports to represent. This depends on many factors including the sampling design, coverage error, nonresponse error, and sampling error.

Fallback statements. Standardized responses for interviewers to provide when asked anticipated questions about the survey by a household gatekeeper or a respondent (e.g., "Where did you get my telephone number?").

Fast-busy. A distinctly different repeating signal occasionally heard after a dialing. It is noticeably more rapid than a normal busy, and often indicates that a number is nonworking or that the dialing did not execute properly.

Gatekeeper. Anyone whom an interviewer must "get past" to speak to a selected respondent. Typically, the gatekeeper is the first person who answers the telephone when that person turns out not to be the selected respondent.

Geographic screening. A series of questions usually asked as part of the introductory/selection sequence that attempts to determine whether or not a given respondent lives within the geographic boundaries of the sampling area of a telephone survey. Geographic screening is subject to errors of omission (false negatives) and errors of commission (false positives) and, therefore, is often impractical to employ.

Hit-rate. The proportion of telephone numbers in a sampling pool that leads to eligible respondents. In a general population survey, the hit-rate is typically the percentage of the sampling pool that reaches residences.

Household informant. Anyone in a household who can provide valid answers to an interviewer about the household; for example, anyone who can accurately report the number of persons living in the household as part of a respondent selection sequence.

Interviewer monitoring form (IMF). A form used by supervisory personnel to structure the monitoring of ongoing interviews. The information recorded on an IMF can provide feedback to interviewers and can be used by a researcher to estimate the size and nature of interviewer-related measurement error.

Interviewer productivity. The number of properly completed interviews attained by an interviewer within a given time frame (e.g., per hour) compared to the number of refusals experienced within the same time frame. In general, a 3:1 completion/refusal ratio is a minimum for which interviewers should strive.

Introduction/selection sheet. A separate sheet of paper, often attached to each call-sheet, containing the introductory spiel and respondent selection technique employed in a survey.

Introductory spiel. The standardized introduction read by an interviewer when contact is made with a possible eligible household or respondent.

Kish selection method. The most rigorous of respondent selection methods, the Kish method is the accepted standard for in-person interviews. It requires a full enumeration of all persons within a sampling unit who meet a survey's eligibility criteria (e.g., person 18 years of age or older). Although considered a true probability selection technique in theory, in practice when used in a telephone survey it does not achieve a truly random within-unit probability sample. Due to its highly intrusive nature at the start of interviewer contact it can lead to especially high refusal rates when used by unskilled interviewers.

Margin of error. See Sampling error.

Measurement error. The portion of total survey error that is due to interviewers' behavior, respondents' behavior, the questionnaire, and/or the mode by which the survey is conducted. To the extent that measurement error cannot be eliminated, given available resources the prudent researcher will build methodological tests into a survey to allow for post hoc investigation of the size of the measurement error.

Mitofsky-Waksberg two-stage RDD sampling. A well-accepted approach to generating an RDD sampling pool that achieves a very high household hit-rate. In the first stage, simple random digit dialing is used to identify a relatively small number of telephone numbers that reach households within the sampling area. These prefixes and typically the first two digits of their accompanying suffix are then used as seeds to generate the second-stage sampling pool. Sampling error is somewhat higher than with a comparable one-stage sampling pool.

Mixed mode payment. Payment of interviewers composed of a fixed hourly wage and a variable productivity bonus.

Mixed mode survey. The use of more than one survey mode (mail, personal, and/or telephone) to gather data for the same survey project. The goal of mixed mode surveys is to take advantage of the particular strengths of the various modes in reducing total survey error while minimizing their respective weaknesses.

Multiple-frame sampling. The use of more than one sampling frame to generate the sampling pool used in a survey; for example, combining random digit dialing with sampling from a reverse directory. The purpose of this approach is to achieve a favorable balance between survey costs and likely errors.

Nondirective probing. Probing ambiguous and otherwise inadequate responses by interviewers in a nonbiasing manner. This technique focuses on the behavior that a respondent exhibits by providing answers to survey questions, rather than on the affect communicated in those answers. An example of a nondirective probe: "Could you be more specific on that last point?"

Nonresponse error. The portion of total survey error due to differences between those elements that are sampled but for which no data are gathered versus those sampled for which data are gathered. Nonresponse in a survey is due to noncontacts and refusals, with the latter composing the majority of nonresponse in most telephone surveys of the public. The magnitude of the nonresponse error is a function of the size of the proportion of the population that was sampled but that was not interviewed and its difference from the proportion that was interviewed. If "nonresponders" do not differ on the measures gathered by a survey from "responders," then there is no nonresponse error.

Nonsampling error. The combined error associated with problems of coverage, measurement, and nonresponse.

On-the-job training. Interviewer training that is achieved via structured feedback from supervisors to interviewers during ongoing interviewing sessions.

Panel survey. Any survey in which the same respondents are interviewed a second time, or more, using the same basic questionnaire at each "wave" of the panel. Panel waves are often conducted at 12 month intervals.

PAPI. Paper-and-pencil-interviewing, in which interviewers read questions from printed questionnaires and record answers directly on the questionnaires.

Pilot test. A relatively small number of practice interviews to test and further refine the efficiency of the sampling pool and the wording of the introduction, selection procedure, and questionnaire. Pilot tests also help determine how long it takes to administer the questionnaire. Typically, a debriefing session is held after the pilot test with those interviewers who participated in it.

Population parameter. A value that represents the level at which some variable exists in a population. Surveys are typically used to estimate these parameters.

Prefix. The first three digits in a local telephone number; also referred to as a local telephone exchange.

Probability sample. Various sampling approaches that theoretically afford a nonzero known probability of selection to every element in the population. Calculation of the magnitude of sampling error is only possible with probability samples.

Quality control. The system used in a survey to enhance the quality of sampling and interviewing, so as to reduce total survey error. In general, telephone surveys afford a greater opportunity for quality control than other survey modes.

Random digit dialing. Several techniques that form sampling pools by adding random digits to prefixes known to ring in the sampling area, so as to make it possible to reach households with unpublished and/or unlisted telephone numbers.

Random numbers table. Table of thousands of digits (0-9) printed in the back of many statistics books. These digits are printed in a random order. Strings of these random digits can be used by survey researchers for various purposes; for example, they can be used to form random suffixes for prefixes that will be used in an RDD sampling pool.

Refusal avoidance training. Intensive training given interviewers on how to try to minimize the number of refusals they experience. The focus of this training is to explain to interviewers the various strategies that appear to be associated with low refusal rates. Practice via role playing is an important component of this training.

Refusal report form (RRF). A structured form used by interviewers each time they experience a refusal. The form can aid subsequent attempts to convert refusals and may aid the researcher in the investigation of the nature of nonresponse error in the survey.

Respondent exclusion criterion. An a priori factor that make a person ineligible to be chosen as a survey respondent; for example, being too young or not speaking English.

Respondent selection. The technique used by interviewers after an introductory spiel to properly choose a respondent from all eligible respondents within a sampling unit.

Response rates. Several approaches to calculating numerical measures (percentages) of the efficiency of a sampling pool in reaching eligible respondents and the efficiency of interviewers in completing interviews with those eligible.

Reverse directory. A special telephone directory with numbers ordered numerically and/or by street address, rather than alphabetically by last names. Unlisted telephone numbers are not included in a reverse directory.

Role playing. An interviewer-training technique in which interviewers practice using a survey's introduction, selection procedure, and questionnaire with supervisory personnel acting the part of the respondent.

Sampling boundaries. The geographic area within which a telephone survey will sample units/respondents.

Sampling design. The plan that guides the selection of a survey sample to represent the population of interest. It identifies the target population, the sampling boundaries, how the sampling pool will be generated from the sampling frame, how respondents will be chosen within a sampling unit, the size of the final sample, and postsampling weighting adjustments.

Sampling error. The portion of total survey error due to the fact that only a sample of all elements in a population are studied rather than a census. Provided that a probability sample is used, the size of the sampling error can be calculated using standard statistical formulas.

Sampling frame. The list of elements in a target population from which the sampling pool is generated. In RDD surveys a sampling frame does not actually exist, rather it exists in theory in the sense that it is composed of all the tens of thousands of telephone numbers that could possibly exist (i.e., suffixes 0000-9999) for each and every prefix that rings within the sampling boundaries.

Sampling pool. The actual set of telephone numbers generated from the sampling frame that will be used by interviewers to reach respondents. In PAPI, every number used from a sampling pool is printed on a separate call-sheet to control its proper processing.

Saturation. As applied to general population telephone surveys, the proportion of households in a sampling area with at least one telephone access line. In the early 1990s, the saturation of telephones in U.S. residences was estimated to be 93%-95%.

Skip pattern. Any sequence of items within a questionnaire that is contingent upon one or more previous answers.

Stratification by prefix. A sampling pool in which telephone numbers are proportionally represented in accordance with the actual prevalence of their prefix within the survey's sampling boundaries.

Suffix. The last four digits of a telephone number.

Sugging. An unethical telemarketing sales technique of "Selling *U*nder the *G*uise" of surveying, in which callers represent themselves as telephone survey interviewers when all along their actual purpose is to deliver a sales pitch. Sugging is thought to have contributed to the growing problem of nonresponse among the general public.

Systematic sampling. Different techniques that can be used to form sampling pools directly from telephone directories or other listings by taking a random start and then using a fixed selection interval to choose the next element in the listing.

Target population. The finite population that is actually sampled.

Total survey error. The bias (constant error) and variance (variable error) in survey findings due to the combined effects of coverage error, nonresponse error, measurement error, and sampling error. To the extent that total survey error cannot be eliminated, it may be possible to measure its size and nature.

Unlisted numbers. Any telephone number that neither is published in a local telephone directory nor will it be given out by directory assistance.

Unpublished numbers. Any telephone number that is not published in a local telephone directory. It may or may not be given out by directory assistance depending on local telephone company procedures.

Vacuous suffix bank. A range of telephone suffixes for a given prefix that contains no working telephone numbers.

Validation. The immediate review of a completed PAPI questionnaire by the supervisory personnel on duty at an interviewing session to determine that the interviewer properly completed the entire questionnaire and recorded open-end responses legibly.

Verification. Calling back a respondent to verify that an interview was in fact completed. Verification is done by supervisory personnel typically within a day or two after the original completion.

Videophone. A telecommunications product that went on sale to the public in 1992. Operating on a regular access line, the technology allows users to see the other person(s) involved in the conversation providing both parties have a videophone. If the technology is embraced by the public, telephone survey-ors will need to research and develop procedures for the use of the technology that minimize its effect on total survey error.

Weighting. Post hoc statistical adjustments of survey data to enhance the external validity, and thus the accuracy, of the survey's estimates of population parameters. It is standard and accepted practice to weight telephone surveys for unequal probabilities of selection due to multiple access lines and the variable number of eligibles within a sampling unit. Commonly used, but not always appropriate, is weighting for demographic differences between the final sample and the population in order to compensate for nonresponse.

Within-unit sampling. The selection of a specified number of eligible respondents, typically one, within a sampling unit (e.g., a household) using a structured respondent selection technique.

References

American Association for Public Opinion Research (AAPOR). (1991). *Code of professional ethics and practices.* Ann Arbor, MI: AAPOR Secretary's Office.

Andrews, E. L. (1992, March 15). Emboldened phone companies are pushing the frills. *New York Times,* p. F8.

Alexander, C. A. (1988). Cutoff rules for secondary calling in a random digit dialing survey. In R. M. Groves, P. P. Biemer, L. E. Lyberg, J. T. Massey, W. L. Nicholls, & J. Waksberg (Eds.), *Telephone survey methodology* (pp. 113-126). New York: John Wiley.

Alexander, C. A., Sebold, J., & Pfaff, P. (1986). Some results with an experiment with telephone sampling for the US national crime survey. *Proceedings of the Section on Survey Research Methods,* American Statistical Association, Chicago.

AT&T. (1982). *The world's telephones: 1982.* Atlanta: R. H. Donnelley.

Babbie, E. (1989). *The practice of social research* (5th ed.). Belmont, CA: Wadsworth.

Baker, R. P., & Lefes, W. L. (1988). The design of CATI systems: A review of current practice. In R. M. Groves, P. P. Biemer, L. E. Lyberg, J. T. Massey, W. L. Nicholls, & J. Waksberg (Eds.), *Telephone survey methodology* (pp. 387-402). New York: John Wiley.

Bass, R. T., & Tortora, R. D. (1988). A comparison of centralized CATI facilities for an agricultural labor survey. In R. M. Groves, P. P. Biemer, L. E. Lyberg, J. T. Massey, W. L. Nicholls, & J. Waksberg (Eds.), *Telephone survey methodology* (pp. 497-508). New York: John Wiley.

Bauman, S. L., Merkle, D. M., & Lavrakas, P. J. (1992). *Interviewer estimates of refusers' gender, age, and race in telephone surveys.* Paper presented at the Midwest Association for Public Opinion Research Conference, Chicago.

Belson, W. A. (1981). *The design and understanding of survey questions.* Aldershot, England: Gower.

Berry, S. H., & O'Rourke, D. (1988). Administrative designs for centralized telephone survey centers: Implications of the transition to CATI. In R. M. Groves, P. P. Biemer, L. E. Lyberg, J. T. Massey, W. L. Nicholls, & J. Waksberg (Eds.), *Telephone survey methodology* (pp. 457-474). New York: John Wiley.

Biemer, P. P., Groves, R. M., Lyberg, L. E., Mathiowetz, N. A., & Sudman, S. (Eds.). (1991). *Measurement errors in surveys.* New York: John Wiley.

Blair J., & Chun, Y. (1992). *Quality of data from converted refusals in telephone surveys.* Paper presented at the American Association for Public Opinion Research Conference, St. Petersburg, FL.

Bradburn, N. M., & Sudman, S. (1991). The current status of questionnaire design. In P. P. Biemer, R. M. Groves, L. E. Lyberg, N. A. Mathiowetz, & S. Sudman (Eds.), *Measurement errors in surveys* (pp. 29-40). New York: John Wiley.

Bradburn, N. M., Sudman, S., & Associates. (1979). *Improving interview method and questionnaire design.* San Francisco: Jossey-Bass.

Brook, J. (1976). *Telephone: The first hundred years.* New York: Harper & Row.

Bryant, B. E. (1975). Respondent selection in a time of changing household composition. *Journal of Marketing Research, 12,* 129-135.

Burkheimer, G. J., & Levinsohn, J. R. (1988). Implementing the Mitofsky-Waksberg sampling design with accelerated sequential replacement. In R. M. Groves, P. P. Biemer, L. E. Lyberg, J. T. Massey, W. L. Nicholls, & J. Waksberg (Eds.), *Telephone survey methodology* (pp. 99-112). New York: John Wiley.

Catlin, G., & Ingram, S. (1988). The effects of CATI on costs and data quality: A comparison of CATI and paper methods in centralized interviewing. In R. M. Groves, P. P. Biemer, L. E. Lyberg, J. T. Massey, W. L. Nicholls, & J. Waksberg (Eds.), *Telephone survey methodology* (pp. 437-452). New York: John Wiley.

Campbell, D. T., & Stanley, J. (1966). *Experimental and quasi-experimental designs for research.* Chicago: Rand McNally.

Cannell, C. (1991, October). *Research on monitoring interviewers' behaviors.* Informal presentation at the Institute for Social Research, University of Michigan.

Cannell, C., & Oksenberg, L. (1988). Observation of behavior in telephone interviews. In R. M. Groves, P. P. Biemer, L. E. Lyberg, J. T. Massey, W. L. Nicholls, & J. Waksberg (Eds.), *Telephone survey methodology* (pp. 475-496). New York: John Wiley.

Cochran, W. G. (1977). *Sampling techniques.* New York: John Wiley.

Collins, M., Sykes, W., Wilson, P., & Blackshaw, N. (1988). Nonresponse: The UK experience. In R. M. Groves, P. P. Biemer, L. E. Lyberg, J. T. Massey, W. L. Nicholls, & J. Waksberg (Eds.), *Telephone survey methodology* (pp. 213-232). New York: John Wiley.

Congressional Information Service (1990). *American statistical index.* Bethesda, MD: CIS.

Cook, T. D., & Campbell, D. T. (1979). *Quasi-experimentation: Designs and analysis issues for field settings.* Chicago: Rand McNally.

Cooper, S. L. (1964). Random sampling by telephone: An improved method. *Journal of Marketing Research, 1*(4), 45-48.

Couper, M. P., Holland, L., & Groves, R. M. (1992). *"Hello my name is . . .": Respondent-interviewer interactions in survey introductions.* Paper presented at the American Association for Public Opinion Research Conference, St. Petersburg, FL.

Czaja, R., Blair, J., & Sebestik, J. (1982). Respondent selection in a telephone survey. *Journal of Marketing Research, 19,* 381-385.

Dawes, R. M. (1972). *Fundamentals of attitude measurement.* New York: John Wiley.

de Leeuw, E. D., & van der Zouwen, J. (1988). Data quality in telephone and face to face surveys: A comparative meta-analysis. In R. M. Groves, P. P. Biemer, L. E. Lyberg, J. T. Massey, W. L. Nicholls, & J. Waksberg (Eds.), *Telephone survey methodology* (pp. 283-300). New York: John Wiley.

de Sola Pool, I. (Ed.). (1977). *The social impact of the telephone.* Cambridge: MIT Press.

Dillman, D. A. (1978). *Mail and telephone surveys: The total design method.* New York: John Wiley.

Dillman, D. A., Gallegos, J., & Frey, J. H. (1976). Reducing refusals for telephone interviews. *Public Opinion Quarterly, 40,* 99-114.

Dillman, D. A., Sangster, R. L., & Rockwood, T. H. (1992). *Question form effects in mail and telephone surveys: Results from 14 experiments.* Paper presented at the American Association for Public Opinion Research Conference, St. Petersburg, FL.

Dillman, D. A., & Tarnai, J. (1988). Administrative issues in mixed mode surveys. In R. M. Groves, P. P. Biemer, L. E. Lyberg, J. T. Massey, W. L. Nicholls, & J. Waksberg (Eds.), *Telephone survey methodology* (pp. 509-528). New York: John Wiley.

Dillman, D. A., & Tarnai, J. (1991). Mode effects of cognitively designed recall questions: A comparison of answers to telephone and mail surveys. In P. P. Biemer, R. M. Groves,

L. E. Lyberg, N. A. Mathiowetz, & S. Sudman (Eds.), *Measurement errors in surveys* (pp. 73-94). New York: John Wiley.

Drew, J. D., Choudhry, G. H., & Hunter, L. A. (1988). Nonresponse issues in government telephone surveys. In R. M. Groves, P. P. Biemer, L. E. Lyberg, J. T. Massey, W. L. Nicholls, & J. Waksberg (Eds.), *Telephone survey methodology* (pp. 233-246). New York: John Wiley.

Ekman, P., & Friesen, W. (1974). Detecting deception from body and face. *Journal of Personality and Social Psychology, 29,* 288-298.

Ekman, P., & Friesen, W. (1976). Body movement and voice pitch in deceptive interaction. *Semiotica, 16,* 23-27.

Fowler, F. J., Jr. (1984). *Survey research methods.* Beverly Hills, CA: Sage.

Fowler, F. J., Jr. (1993). *Survey research methods* (2nd ed.). Newbury Park, CA: Sage.

Fowler, F. J., Jr., & Mangione, T. W. (1985). *The value of interviewer training and supervision.* Final Report to the National Center for Health Services Research, Washington, DC.

Fowler, F. J., Jr., & Mangione, T. W. (1986). *Reducing interviewer effects on health survey data.* Washington, DC: National Center for Health Statistics.

Fowler, F. J., Jr., & Mangione, T. W. (1990). *Standardized survey interviewing.* Newbury Park, CA: Sage.

Frey, J. H. (1989). *Survey research by telephone* (2nd ed.). Newbury Park, CA: Sage.

Gawiser, S. R., & Witt, G. E. (1992). *Twenty questions a journalist should ask about poll results.* New York: National Council on Public Polls.

Groves, R. M. (1989). *Survey errors and survey costs.* New York: John Wiley.

Groves, R. M., Biemer, P. P., Lyberg, L. E., Massey, J. T., Nicholls, W. L., & Waksberg, J. (Eds.). (1988). *Telephone survey methodology.* New York: John Wiley.

Groves, R. M., & Kahn, R. L. (1979). *Surveys by telephone: A national comparison with personal interviews.* New York: Academic Press.

Groves, R. M., & Lyberg, L. E. (1988). An overview of nonresponse issues in telephone surveys. In R. M. Groves, P. P. Biemer, L. E. Lyberg, J. T. Massey, W. L. Nicholls, & J. Waksberg (Eds.), *Telephone survey methodology* (pp. 191-212). New York: John Wiley.

Hagen, D. E., & Collier, C. M. (1982). Must respondent selection procedures for telephone surveys be invasive? *Public Opinion Quarterly, 47,* 547-556.

Hays, W. L. (1973). *Statistics for the social sciences.* New York: Holt, Rinehart & Winston.

Hedrick, T., Bickman, L., & Rog, D. (1993). *Applied research design.* Newbury Park, CA: Sage.

Henry, G. T. (1990). *Practical sampling.* Newbury Park, CA: Sage.

House, C. C., & Nicholls, W. L. (1988). Questionnaire design for CATI: Design objectives and methods. In R. M. Groves, P. P. Biemer, L. E. Lyberg, J. T. Massey, W. L. Nicholls, & J. Waksberg (Eds.), *Telephone survey methodology* (pp. 421-436). New York: John Wiley.

Kish, L. (1949). A procedure for objective respondent selection within the household. *Journal of the American Statistical Association, 44,* 380-387.

Kish, L. (1962). Studies of interviewer variance for attitudinal variables. *Journal of the American Statistical Association, 57,* 92-115.

Kish, L. (1965). *Survey sampling.* New York: John Wiley.

Kviz, F. J. (1977). Towards a standard definition of response rate. *Public Opinion Quarterly, 41,* 265-267.

Landon, E. L., & Banks, S. K. (1977). Relative efficiency and bias of plus-one telephone sampling. *Journal of Marketing Research, 14,* 294-299.

Lavrakas, P. J. (1987). *Telephone survey methods: Sampling, selection, and supervision.* Newbury Park, CA: Sage.

Lavrakas, P. J. (1990). *Morton Grove district 70 enrollment study* [Mimeo]. Evanston, IL: Northwestern University Survey Lab.

Lavrakas, P. J. (1991). Implementing CATI at the Northwestern Survey Lab: Part I. *CATI News, 4*(1), 2-3+.

Lavrakas, P. J. (1992). *Attitudes towards and experiences with sexual harassment in the workplace.* Paper presented at the Midwest Association for Public Opinion Research Conference, Chicago.

Lavrakas, P. J., & Maier, R. A. (1979). Differences in human ability to judge veracity from the audio medium. *Journal of Research in Personality, 13,* 139-153.

Lavrakas, P. J., & Merkle, D. M. (1991). *A reversal of roles: When respondents question interviewers.* Paper presented at the Midwest Association for Public Opinion Research Conference, Chicago.

Lavrakas, P. J., Merkle, D. M., & Bauman, S. L. (1992). *Refusal report forms, refusal conversions, and nonresponse bias.* Paper presented at the American Association for Public Opinion Research Conference, St. Petersburg, FL.

Lavrakas, P. J., Merkle, D. M., & Bauman, S. L. (1993). *The last-birthday selection method and within-unit coverage problems.* Paper presented at the American Association for Public Opinion Research Conference, St. Charles, IL.

Lavrakas, P. J., & Rosenbaum, D. P. (1989). *Crime prevention beliefs, policies and practices of chief law enforcement executives: Results of national study.* Washington, DC: National Crime Prevention Council.

Lavrakas, P. J., Settersten, R. A., Jr., & Maier, R. A., Jr. (1991). RDD panel attrition in two local area surveys. *Survey Methodology, 17,* 143-152.

Lavrakas, P. J., Skogan, W. G., Normoyle, J., Herz, E. J., Salem, G., & Lewis, D. A. (1980). *Factors related to citizen participation in personal, household, and neighborhood anti-crime measures* [Mimeo]. Evanston, IL: Center for Urban Affairs & Policy Research.

Lavrakas, P. J., & Tyler, T. R. (1983). *Low cost telephone surveys.* Paper presented at Evaluation '83, Chicago.

LeBailly, R. F., & Lavrakas, P. J. (1981). *Generating a random digit dialing sample for telephone surveys.* Paper presented at Issue '81 Annual SPSS Convention, San Francisco.

Lepkowski, J. M. (1988). Telephone sampling methods in the United States. In R. M. Groves, P. P. Biemer, L. E. Lyberg, J. T. Massey, W. L. Nicholls, & J. Waksberg (Eds.), *Telephone survey methodology* (pp. 73-98). New York: John Wiley.

Lewis, I. A. (1991). Media polls, the *Los Angeles Times* poll, and the 1988 presidential election. In P. J. Lavrakas & J. K. Holley (Eds.), *Polling and presidential election coverage* (pp. 57-82). Newbury Park, CA: Sage.

Lipsey, M. W. (1989). *Design sensitivity: Statistical power for experimental research.* Newbury Park, CA: Sage.

Lyberg, L. E. (1988). Introduction: The administration of telephone surveys. In R. M. Groves, P. P. Biemer, L. E. Lyberg, J. T. Massey, W. L. Nicholls, & J. Waksberg (Eds.), *Telephone survey methodology* (pp. 453-456). New York: John Wiley.

Lyberg, L. E., & Dean, P. (1992). *Methods for reducing nonresponse rates—a review.* Paper presented at the American Association for Public Opinion Research Conference, St. Petersburg, FL.

Maier, N.R.F. (1966). Sensitivity to attempts at deception in an interview situation. *Personnel Psychology, 19,* 55-66.

Maier, N.R.F., & Thurber, J. (1968). Accuracy of judgments of deception when an interview is watched, heard or read. *Personnel Psychology, 21,* 23-30.

Maier, R. A., & Lavrakas, P. J. (1976). Lying behavior and evaluation of lies. *Perceptual and Motor Skills, 42,* 575-581.

Maklan, D., & Waksberg, J. (1988). Within-household coverage in RDD surveys. In R. M. Groves, P. P. Biemer, L. E. Lyberg, J. T. Massey, W. L. Nicholls, & J. Waksberg (Eds.), *Telephone survey methodology* (pp. 51-72). New York: John Wiley.

Mason, R. E., & Immerman, F. W. (1988). Minimum cost sample allocation for Mitofsky-Waksberg random digit dialing. In R. M. Groves, P. P. Biemer, L. E. Lyberg, J. T. Massey, W. L. Nicholls, & J. Waksberg (Eds.), *Telephone survey methodology* (pp. 127-142). New York: John Wiley.

Massey, J. T. (1988). An overview of telephone coverage. In R. M. Groves, P. P. Biemer, L. E. Lyberg, J. T. Massey, W. L. Nicholls, & J. Waksberg (Eds.), *Telephone survey methodology* (pp. 3-8). New York: John Wiley.

Massey, J. T., & Botman, S. L. (1988). Weighting adjustments for random digit dialed surveys. In R. M. Groves, P. P. Biemer, L. E. Lyberg, J. T. Massey, W. L. Nicholls, & J. Waksberg (Eds.), *Telephone survey methodology* (pp. 143-160). New York: John Wiley.

Merkle, D. M., Bauman, S. L., & Lavrakas, P. J. (1991). *Nonresponse bias: Refusal conversions and call-backs in RDD telephone surveys.* Paper presented at the Midwest Association for Public Opinion Research Conference, Chicago.

Mitofsky, W. J. (1970). *Sampling of telephone households* [Mimeo]. New York: CBS News.

Nicholls, W. L. (1988). Computer-assisted telephone interviewing: A general introduction. In R. M. Groves, P. P. Biemer, L. E. Lyberg, J. T. Massey, W. L. Nicholls, & J. Waksberg (Eds.), *Telephone Survey Methodology* (pp. 377-386). New York: John Wiley.

Oldendick, R. W., Sorenson, S. B., Tuchfarber, A. J., & Bishop, G. F. (1985). *Last birthday respondent selection in telephone surveys: A further test.* Paper presented at Midwest Association of Public Opinion Research, Chicago.

Oksenberg, L., & Cannell, C. (1988). Effects of interviewer vocal characteristics on nonresponse. In R. M. Groves, P. P. Biemer, L. E. Lyberg, J. T. Massey, W. L. Nicholls, & J. Waksberg (Eds.), *Telephone survey methodology* (pp. 257-272). New York: John Wiley.

O'Rourke, D., & Blair, J. (1983). Improving random respondent selection in telephone surveys. *Journal of Marketing Research, 20,* 428-432.

Pierce, J. R. (1977). The telephone and society in the past 100 years. In I. de Sola Pool (Ed.), *The social impact of the telephone* (pp. 159-195). Cambridge: MIT Press.

Potthoff, R. F. (1987). Some generalizations of the Mitofsky-Waksberg technique for random digit dialing. *Journal of the American Statistical Association, 82,* 409-418.

Ramirez, A. (1992, April 30). Lifetime telephone numbers that ring anywhere you go. *New York Times,* p. A1+.

Robinson, J. P., Shaver, P. R., & Wrightsman, L. W. (1991). *Measures of personality and social psychological attitudes.* New York: Academic Press.

Salmon, C. T., & Nichols, J. S. (1983). The next-birthday method for respondent selection. *Public Opinion Quarterly, 47,* 270-276.

Schuman, H., & Presser, S. (1981). *Questions and answers in attitude surveys.* New York: Academic Press.

Sebold, J. (1988). Survey period length, unanswered numbers, and nonresponse in telephone surveys. In R. M. Groves, P. P. Biemer, L. E. Lyberg, J. T. Massey, W. L. Nicholls, & J. Waksberg (Eds.), *Telephone survey methodology* (pp. 247-256). New York: John Wiley.

Smead, R. J., & Wilcox, J. (1980). Ring policy in telephone surveys. *Public Opinion Quarterly, 44,* 115-116.

Stokes, L., & Ming-Yih, Y. (1988). Searching for causes of interviewer effects in telephone surveys. In R. M. Groves, P. P. Biemer, L. E. Lyberg, J. T. Massey, W. L. Nicholls, & J. Waksberg (Eds.), *Telephone survey methodology* (pp. 357-376). New York: John Wiley.

Sudman, S. (1973). The uses of telephone directories for survey sampling. *Journal of Marketing Research, 10* (May), 204-207.

Sudman, S. (1976). *Applied sampling.* New York: Academic Press.

Sudman, S., & Bradburn, N. (1974). *Response effects in surveys: A review and synthesis.* Chicago: Aldine.

Sudman, S., & Bradburn, N. (1982). *Asking questions.* San Francisco: Jossey-Bass.

Survey Sampling, Inc. (1990). *A survey researcher's view of the U.S.* Fairfield, CT: Survey Sampling.

Thornberry, O. T., Jr., & Massey, J. T. (1988). Trends in United States telephone coverage across time and subgroups. In R. M. Groves, P. P. Biemer, L. E. Lyberg, J. T. Massey, W. L. Nicholls, & J. Waksberg (Eds.), *Telephone survey methodology* (pp. 25-50). New York: John Wiley.

Traugott, M. R. (1987). The importance of persistence in respondent selection for preelection surveys. *Public Opinion Quarterly, 51,* 48-57.

Traugott, M. R., Groves, R. M., & Lepkowski, J. (1987). Using dual frame designs to reduce nonresponse in telephone surveys. *Public Opinion Quarterly, 51,* 522-539.

Trewin, D., & Lee, G. (1988). International comparisons of telephone coverage. In R. M. Groves, P. P. Biemer, L. E. Lyberg, J. T. Massey, W. L. Nicholls, & J. Waksberg (Eds.), *Telephone survey methodology* (pp. 9-24). New York: John Wiley.

Troldahl, V. C., & Carter, R. E., Jr. (1964). Random selection of respondents within households in phone surveys. *Journal of Marketing Research, 1,* 71-76.

Tucker, C. (1983). Interviewer effects in telephone surveys. *Public Opinion Quarterly, 47,* 84-95.

U.S. Bureau of Census (1984). *Statistical abstracts of the United States, 1984.* Washington, DC: Government Printing Office.

Waksberg, J. (1978). Sampling methods for random digit dialing. *Journal of the American Statistical Association, 73,* 40-46.

Weeks, M. F. (1988). Call scheduling with CATI: Current capabilities and methods. In R. M. Groves, P. P. Biemer, L. E. Lyberg, J. T. Massey, W. L. Nicholls, & J. Waksberg (Eds.), *Telephone survey methodology* (pp. 403-420). New York: John Wiley.

Weeks, M. F., Jones, B. L., Folsom, R. E., & Benrud, C. H. (1980). Optimal times to contact sample households. *Public Opinion Quarterly, 44,* 101-114.

Weeks, M. F., Kulka, R. A., & Pierson, S. (1987). Optimal call scheduling for a telephone survey. *Public Opinion Quarterly, 51,* 540-549.

Weiss, C. (1972). *Evaluation research.* Englewood Cliffs, NJ: Prentice-Hall.

Wolter, K. (1985). *Introduction to variance estimation.* New York: Springer Verlag.

Index